Thin

For B. W.

Thinking of You

A resource for the spiritual care of people with dementia

Joanna Collicutt

The Bible Reading Fellowship
15 The Chambers, Vineyard
Abingdon OX14 3FE
brf.org.uk

The Bible Reading Fellowship (BRF) is a Registered Charity (233280)

ISBN 978 0 85746 491 0
First published 2017
10 9 8 7 6 5 4 3 2 1 0

Acknowledgements
Unless otherwise stated, all Bible quotations are from the New Revised Standard
Version Bible, copyright © 1989 the Division of Christian Education of the
National Council of the Churches of Christ in the United States of America. Used
by permission. All rights reserved. • Bible quotations marked (GNT) are from the
Good News Translation. Copyright © 1992 by American Bible Society. • Scripture
quotations taken from The Holy Bible, New International Version (Anglicised edition)
copyright © 1979, 1984, 2011 by Biblica. Used by permission of Hodder & Stoughton
Publishers, a Hachette UK company. All rights reserved. 'NIV' is a registered
trademark of Biblica. UK trademark number 1448790. • Extracts from The Book of
Common Prayer of 1662, the rights of which are vested in the Crown in perpetuity
within the United Kingdom, are reproduced by permission of Cambridge University
Press, Her Majesty's Printers.

Extract on p. 109 'Prayer' © Brian Thorne (2013). In *Accompaniment to a Life* (The
Norwich Centre), p. 14. Used with kind permission. • Poem on p. 144 © Doug Chaplin.
Used with kind permission. • Poem on p. 178 © Richard Underwood. The poem is
from his 'Dreams of the Soul Poetry Anthology' available free from https://www.
smashwords.com/books/view/606870. Used with kind permission.

p. 24: electron microscope image of neurons with amyloid plaques © Thinkstock;
illustrations on pp. 18, 20, 32–36, 40 and 75 by Laszlo Veres (Beehive Illustration);
p. 37: photomicrograph of Lewy bodies © Suraj Rajan, licensed under CC 3.0.

Every effort has been made to trace and contact copyright owners for material used
in this resource. We apologise for any inadvertent omissions or errors, and would
ask those concerned to contact us so that full acknowledgement can be made in
the future.

A catalogue record for this book is available from the British Library

Printed and bound by CPI Group (UK) Ltd, Croydon CR0 4YY

Contents

Foreword 7

About this book 9

Acknowledgements 10

Part 1: Thinking about dementia 11

Chapter 1 A medical approach to dementia: 'Old-timer's disease'? ... 14

Chapter 2 A biological approach to dementia: the fading brain 29

Chapter 3 A social approach to dementia: not gone but forgotten 43

Part 2: Thinking about the person with dementia 57

Chapter 4 I think therefore I am? 59

Chapter 5 Beyond 'I think therefore I am' 70

Chapter 6 God thinks therefore I am 81

Part 3: Thinking of you: the spiritual care of people with dementia 93

Chapter 7 Being present to the person with dementia 98

Chapter 8 Meaning-making in dementia 111

Chapter 9 Re-membering the person with dementia 125

Part 4: Thinking about us: dementia-friendly churches 140

Chapter 10 Full inclusion 144

Chapter 11 Real belonging 154

Chapter 12 Celebration 167

Chapter 13 Connection 183

Chapter 14 Safe enough to play 193

Foreword
by the Bishop of Dorchester

There are at least three reasons why I wish this lovely, thoughtful, spiritual, pastoral, professional and perceptive book had been available many years ago.

The first is that I was vicar of Holy Trinity Margate for eight years in the 1980s. Not surprisingly, given the demographic profile of the town, and of a significant percentage of the congregation, there were a large number of people living with dementia. Some lived with it in themselves, and others as spouses and carers. But, whoever they were, this had major consequences for the pattern of their lives. Looking back, I think we, as a church, could have responded much better than we did. A huge amount of help was provided, but we could have been much more intentional in our response, and Joanna's book would have helped us a great deal in achieving this, to the benefit of all concerned.

Secondly, as for many of my generation, the big 'D' now stands alongside the big 'C' in generating worry and fear. Again I found this book an enormous help in that Joanna so carefully distinguishes between the normal process of ageing, including memory loss, and dementia. But, more than that, her approach to the 'fourth age' is very refreshing. It is all too easy just to label it as a time of diminishment and to miss what can be appreciated and celebrated.

But my third reason is much more personal. My own mother lived with dementia for a number of years before she died. It was very distressing to see the person I had known for so long seeming to fade away. Like so many others, I found it very difficult to cope with, and failed to respond in ways that she and I would have found benefited both of us. While this book would not have changed what we were facing together, it would have helped me a great deal in my response over the years.

So, if you are a leader of a church, or a member of a congregation, that has a large number of people living with dementia; or if you wonder what the future may hold for you as the years creep on; or if dementia is part of your lived experience—my hope and prayer is that these pages will be of benefit both to you and to those around you.

Rt Revd Colin Fletcher
Bishop of Dorchester

August 2016

About this book

Some years ago, in a move that was ahead of its time, Bishop Richard Harries set aside funds within the Diocese of Oxford for ministry among older people. This project came to be called 'Spiritual Care for Older People' (SCOP). The work of SCOP addresses several aspects of the spirituality of ageing, one of which is living well with dementia.

This book is a joint project between the Diocese of Oxford and the Bible Reading Fellowship, and it puts in one place the material that I have used in SCOP training on dementia with churches in Oxfordshire, Berkshire and Buckinghamshire over the last five years. In some of my training sessions, people have been interested in the theological questions raised by dementia; in others, they have wanted to know how to make their churches more dementia-friendly; most often, people seem to want to know more about the condition itself. Dementia still seems to be a mystery to many, and knowing more about what it is takes away some of the fear.

This book covers all of these topics in a logical order, and it makes most sense to start at the beginning and work through. However, if you are anything like me, you may want to dip into the chapters that interest you, and it is possible to do this as they are relatively self-contained. If you can't be doing with theory and want to get straight to the practical tips, then these can be found in Part 4. When reading those chapters that refer to government legislation (particularly Chapters 3 and 14) please be aware that this often varies between the different parts of the UK and is in a continuous process of development, so it is wise to follow weblinks for updates.

Acknowledgements

Many people are supportive of SCOP and its work. I would like to thank Bishop Richard Harries for his foresight in recognising and funding this area of ministry; Bishop Colin Fletcher for his continuing support and advice; and Richard Fisher from BRF for his vision for resourcing the spiritual journey of older people, and his desire to work collaboratively with the Diocese of Oxford. The members of the SCOP steering group—Felicity Blair, Amanda Gafford, Sally Richards and Martin Peirce—offer encouragement, direction and prayer, and I am both needful of and grateful for them. Clergy colleagues, academics and friends have given me ideas, pointed me in the direction of resources and shown me 'how to do it': Alastair Blaine, Dawn Caulfield, Bleddyn Davies, Joy Hance, Jeff Leonardi, Rosemary Peirce, Elizabeth Thomson and particularly Margaret Whipp, who came up with the phrase 'thinking of you'.

Above all, my thanks go to Alison Webster, the Social Responsibility Adviser for the Diocese of Oxford, whose passion for social justice, humility and sheer kindness are inspirational, and without whose patient support this book would not have been written.

Part 1

Thinking about dementia

Dementia seems to be all around us. It's there when we turn on the television or radio news bulletins, or open our daily papers. Most of us could name celebrities who have been affected by dementia—Omar Sharif, Prunella Scales, Margaret Thatcher, Ronald Reagan, Iris Murdoch, Terry Pratchett and so on. Closer to home, dementia is likely to have touched the lives of some of our family members, friends or acquaintances.

But what exactly is it?

The word 'dementia' literally means a loss of mental faculties (from the Latin *mens*, which means mind). It's an effective shorthand word but it doesn't in itself tell us very much. Think for a moment about someone you know who has dementia and ask yourself how many of the following apply to him or her:

- problems in thinking or remembering
- being elderly
- having a medical diagnosis such as Alzheimer's disease
- taking prescribed medications
- depending on others for personal care
- showing aggressive or other challenging behaviour
- withdrawal from previous roles and responsibilities in the community
- absence from social and family gatherings
- financial pressures due to care bills
- close relations who are suffering from stress
- vulnerability to exploitation and abuse
- living in a specialist residential care setting

This exercise should give you a sense of the many things that can be covered by the word 'dementia'. It is not as simple as it may first appear, and there are a number of ways of looking at it.

Most people take the view that dementia is a kind of *illness* with a biological cause (like cancer). On this view, it is important to find ways of diagnosing it accurately and to pursue medical research aimed at developing a cure.

Some take the view that dementia is a particular form of ageing that involves unusually severe cognitive decline, seeing it more as a sort of psychological *disability* (like autism). On this view we might want to be a bit more cautious about saying that an affected individual is 'ill', and instead of talking about a cure we would focus on managing the disability.

Others view dementia as *something that happens to a social group*— to a couple or family, not just to the person who is identified as the 'patient'. On this view 'those affected by dementia' doesn't just mean individuals with the diagnosis, but every member of their social circles who are touched by its effects.

Yet others would take a more radical position and point to the way that societies label, marginalise and even incarcerate some individuals whom they see as no longer useful, or whose very existence challenges their values. (For example the modern age has placed a high value on rational thought, and this means that it cannot really accommodate those who can no longer think rationally.) On this view, dementia is *something that societies do to individuals*.

This book acknowledges that there are elements of truth in all these views (and also some problems with each of them). In fact, we need them all—the biomedical, psychological and social—to do dementia full justice. And there is more: any condition that involves the mental faculties is likely to have a deep *spiritual* impact. Indeed, in our society many people assume that the mind *is* the spirit. That's one reason we find dementia so challenging: if the mind has gone, has the spirit also flown?

While the different sections of the book each focus on these different aspects of dementia, the book as a whole brings them all together, seeing dementia as something that affects the whole of human life, structured around 'thinking of'. Part 1 lays some basic foundations by looking at dementia from a biomedical and social point of view. These foundations need to be in place if we are to explore 'ultimate' questions about the sense of identity and spiritual life of the affected person that form the focus of Part 2. Parts 3 and 4 have a practical emphasis: Part 3 looks at the principles and effective practice of spiritual care of individuals with dementia; Part 4 goes wider and looks at how churches can become more 'dementia-friendly' by reaching out to, welcoming and valuing all affected by dementia.

Chapter 1

A medical approach to dementia: 'old-timer's disease'

When she was a little girl, our daughter misheard the phrase 'Alzheimer's disease' as 'old-timer's disease'. It was an understandable mistake. On the basis of her experience with grandparents and older members of our church congregation, she had got the idea that when people grow old their thinking becomes slow; they become hard of hearing and so do not always 'get' what is going on; they repeat the same stories; they seem set in their ways; they easily mislay items or get into a muddle; and they forget the words for quite simple things, including the names of their own grandchildren! She thought this (or something quite like it) was what people meant when they spoke of dementia.

Most experts would say that these sorts of familiar, age-related changes are *not* dementia, and that dementia is quite distinct from 'normal ageing'. Furthermore, it is possible to develop dementia in early adulthood or midlife, so it isn't simply about being elderly.

Nevertheless, it's hard to distinguish between the early stages of dementia and just being a typical 'old-timer'. This is why specialist tests are needed to make a diagnosis. There is actually a lot of overlap between the problems experienced by older people who will go on to develop dementia and those who won't.

This talk of abnormality, disease and diagnosis tells us that we are entering medical territory, and in this chapter we will take a medical approach to understanding dementia.

Dementia is a symptom

In medical terms, dementia is a symptom (or group of symptoms) rather than a disease.[1] Just as a fever tells us all is not well with the body, dementia tells us all is not well with the brain. But, while fever is simple to measure with a thermometer, dementia is more complex. It is usually described as a *gradual, irreversible decline in mental abilities*— it has a time course. So, to be sure it really is dementia, we need to see if the problem changes over time, either naturally or in response to simple treatment.

If a person gets confused and muddled but this doesn't last very long, then this isn't dementia. If we can find a simple way to treat the person, such as giving sufficient fluids, and the confusion disappears, then it isn't dementia. If a person shows a decline in cognition[2] but this stabilises and does not get worse for several years, then this is not dementia. But if the problem goes on for some time, doesn't respond to simple treatment and is getting progressively worse, we can say it is dementia.

Ageism: don't assume it's dementia

It is easy to jump too quickly to the conclusion that someone has dementia, especially if he or she is elderly. If a young adult becomes confused, disorientated and agitated we are likely to assume that illicit drugs or excessive alcohol are to blame; yet with an older person we will readily consider dementia. This is simply ageism: older people get drunk too! They also take quite a lot of *prescription medication and this can sometimes have unwanted side effects* that impact on cognition.

More importantly, older people can be prone to temporary bouts of confusion that do not signify dementia. Other health conditions such as thyroid problems can mimic dementia. Like young children, older people are very sensitive to *changes in their body physiology*. In hot weather they can easily become dehydrated, and this can make them confused. If they have a chest infection, a urinary tract infection or another type of infection, this can also make them confused. Indeed, confusion may be the first sign that an infection is brewing. As their physiology returns to normal, thanks to hydration or antibiotics, so their cognition returns to normal. They often have no idea they have been confused and there is usually no need to mention it at all; it can be distressing and embarrassing to think you lost control of your own behaviour, even if only for a while.

Depression is a less obvious but nevertheless significant problem. Those of us who have experienced depression will know that when it hits it can be very difficult to think straight, remember information and make decisions. Depression also slows us down. These cognitive impairments can persist unchanged for quite a while if the depression isn't treated, but can be reversed once treatment takes effect. Depression is common in all age groups and is a particular feature of old age. This is probably because people are more likely to experience significant bereavements and other losses in later life. This, together with difficulty in getting out and about to social gatherings, leads to loneliness. Health problems, including poorly managed pain, play their part in lowering mood. It is estimated that one in five older people living in the community is affected by depression, and this rises to one in four of the residential care home population. Yet, many older people do not get the treatment for depression that they need and deserve. This is partly due to ageism again. There is an unfortunately common attitude that depression is a normal part of ageing—surely it must be depressing to get old. Depression is also missed due to the tendency among both ordinary people and some healthcare professionals to jump to the conclusion that an older person who is having persistent problems with thinking must be developing dementia. But depression should always be considered. It is a treatable health condition (medication and/or talking therapies are very effective) and therefore the cognitive problems that go with it are reversible. They do not signify dementia.

Finally, the effects of *age-related hearing loss* (an extremely common condition) can look rather like dementia. The person doesn't follow the conversation, appears to have forgotten what he has been told, gets defensive when challenged and may become socially withdrawn. It is sensible to organise a hearing test or to check out the batteries in an existing hearing aid before considering dementia as an explanation.

Dementia is a symptom *of* something

Even when we are sure that dementia—gradual, irreversible decline in cognitive function—is present, we have only described the symptom. We need to find out what is behind it. Dementia tells us that all is not well with the brain—that there is some sort of process at work that is gradually making more and more of its parts weaken and die. Essentially this is down to either brain sickness or brain starvation (see Figure 1). You could say that that dementia happens either because the brain is diseased or because its energy and oxygen supply are gradually being cut off.

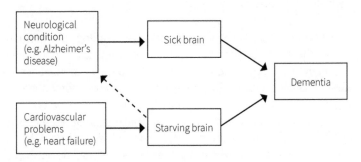

Figure 1 Flow chart showing how a sick or starving brain leads to dementia.

Brain sickness: dementia as a symptom of a progressive neurological condition

Neurological conditions are disorders that affect parts of the nervous system (the brain, the spinal cord and the nerves that are all over and inside our body—see Figure 2).

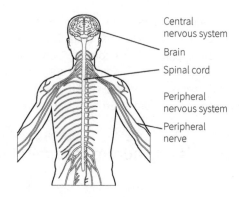

Figure 2 The nervous system.

People with neurological conditions may have problems in any area of human functioning. They can experience difficulties with movement and physical sensation, changes in their emotions, impaired cognition or all of these, depending on what parts of the nervous system are affected. A neurological condition is described as 'progressive' if it gradually gets worse over time.

Dementia only happens when a progressive neurological condition affects the parts of the brain concerned with cognition. Some progressive neurological conditions have a relatively minor impact on these parts; others have a major impact. For example, motor neurone disease has a minimal impact because it primarily affects parts of the brain to do with movement rather than thinking; multiple sclerosis sometimes has a significant impact; Parkinson's disease often has a significant impact; and Alzheimer's disease has a major impact. So, as illustrated in Table 1, dementia is rare in motor neurone disease and multiple sclerosis; it is more common in Parkinson's disease; but it is the defining feature of Alzheimer's disease.

Table 1 Simplified summary of motor and cognitive problems in selected neurological conditions

Progressive neurological condition	Problems with movement	Problems with thinking
Motor neurone disease	Very severe	Relatively mild
Multiple sclerosis	Mild to very severe	Usually mild, but sometimes significant
Parkinson's disease	Significant to very severe	Moderate to significant
Alzheimer's disease	Mild	Significant to very severe

Of all the progressive neurological conditions, it is Alzheimer's disease that is most strongly identified with dementia, and which accounts for the majority of diagnosed dementia cases (about 60%). However, there are some other rarer conditions that are also important—for example Pick's disease (now more commonly known as frontotemporal dementia), Korsakoff's syndrome, Creutzfeldt-Jakob disease (related to BSE) and Lewy body disease.

Brain starvation: dementia as a symptom of a cardiovascular condition

The brain needs oxygen to survive, and brain cells die very quickly if deprived of oxygen. Even if there is no progressive neurological condition at work and the brain itself is basically healthy, dementia can occur because of a disruption to the supply of its oxygen and nutrients. Like the rest of the body, the brain receives oxygen and nutrients such as glucose from the blood vessels that penetrate all its parts (see Figure 3).

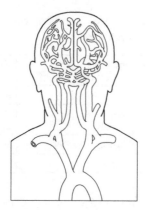

Figure 3 Blood vessels.

If the blood supply to certain parts of the brain is deficient then those parts will weaken or die. This can happen when there are problems with the cardiovascular system—with the heart's ability to keep pumping blood effectively, or with the arteries' and veins' capacity to transport the blood to where it is needed. Where a person is living with a cardiovascular condition such as chronic heart failure, this will often lead to progressive decline in brain function, and dementia can result.

This sort of dementia is referred to as 'vascular dementia', for obvious reasons. It is less common than dementia arising from Alzheimer's disease, accounting for 15–20% of diagnosed dementia cases. However, it is also possible to have both Alzheimer's disease and vascular dementia (and, as indicated by the dashed arrow in Figure 1, cardiovascular disease is a risk factor for Alzheimer's disease); about 10% of diagnosed cases are of this mixed type.

How common is dementia?

It is hard to get a precise figure for the number of people living with dementia because many may keep their condition secret, or it may be missed by doctors if the affected person also has other, more dramatic, physical health conditions. The Alzheimer's Society estimates that about 800,000 people are currently living with dementia in the UK.

Cases of all types of dementia increase with age. Dementia is very rare under the age of 60 (about one in 1400 at any one time). Over 60 the prevalence[3] increases to about one in 100; over 70 to one in 25; over 80 to one in six; over 90 to about one in three.[4] These figures remind us of the important fact that, in the UK at least, *most older people do not have dementia*, and this is true even for the oldest of the old. The prevalence is comparable to that of depression, a much less visible condition.

It appears that the incidence of dementia is steadily increasing. This may be because more people are surviving into old age, or it may be that there is something distinctive about the baby boomer generation (born between 1946 and 1964) that is making it particularly susceptible to dementia. The generation that lived through World War II was a particularly healthy one, forced by circumstances to consume moderate amounts of an organic diet low in refined carbohydrate. But their children came on to the scene when rationing was ending and processed foods were entering the diet. These foods were high in sugar and fat, with chemical additives, and they were produced by farms that were freely employing newly developed pesticides and insecticides. (It is shocking to realise that DDT, a synthetic insecticide now known to have adverse environmental and health effects, was widely used in domestic settings in the 1950s—my mother kept a tin with the cleaning products by the kitchen sink.) It is possible that the post-baby-boomer generations will be healthier, as they have reaped the benefit of legislation controlling additives and other potentially harmful agents in the food chain. If this is so, the steady increase in cases of dementia may flatten out; but only time will tell.

What are the risk factors for dementia?

Apart from *advancing age* and *poor general health*, the environmental risk factors for developing dementia are poorly understood. Obviously, in the case of vascular dementia, the risk factors are effectively the same as for cardiovascular disease (smoking, overconsumption of alcohol, excessive weight, lack of exercise and poor diet). Less obviously, this turns out also to be the case for Alzheimer's disease. So the best protection is to keep physically fit and healthy.

Women are somewhat more likely than men to develop Alzheimer's disease, even allowing for the fact that they live longer.

Genes may also play a part. There are some conditions (such as Huntington's disease) that are entirely genetically determined, but the genetics of Alzheimer's disease is much more complex. Your chance of developing Alzheimer's disease if one of your close relatives has been affected is about twice that of someone with no family history of Alzheimer's—but that means the risk in your 80s is still only about one in three. Early-onset Alzheimer's disease (before the age of 60) is more closely linked to genes so the risk is correspondingly greater for people with a close relative with this form. The genetics of vascular dementia are not well understood.

Overall, the group of people most at risk for developing Alzheimer's disease are *adults with Down's syndrome* aged over 50. This seems to be directly related to their genetic make-up, and clearly poses specific and very significant challenges.

As we have seen, *depression* is a health condition that is quite distinct from dementia, but it does appear that being depressed may put people at somewhat greater risk of developing dementia. Looking at this the other way round, it is essential to be aware that, just as it's possible to have a broken leg, toothache,[5] hearing loss or flu if you have dementia, it's also possible—and quite common—for people with dementia to become depressed. It's not always 'either/or'. Being miserable is not an inevitable consequence of dementia, and not all the distress and confusion experienced by a person with dementia may be down to the dementia alone. This has important practical implications. Possible causes of the depression should be investigated: a person with dementia may become depressed because her care needs are not being properly met, or even because of abuse. Treatments for the depression should also always be explored.

Making a diagnosis: Alzheimer's disease isn't like measles

In the developed world, specialist dementia clinics are burgeoning. There are about 200 in England alone. Their main concern is 'diagnosis'—establishing whether or not the cognitive problems that an individual is experiencing signify dementia, and identifying the underlying health condition. The logic of this sounds simple, but it is far from that. It turns out that diagnosing dementia is much more of an art than a science, even though a lot of scientific-looking procedures are involved. This is because there is no simple and certain test for the most common cause of dementia, Alzheimer's disease. A single blood test is usually sufficient to confirm the diagnosis of an infection such as measles or hepatitis. But Alzheimer's disease isn't an infection; it's a process that affects the brain and the mind.

We might think that the way to establish a diagnosis would be to examine the brain of the affected individual. Brain scans are useful here. They can show how much the brain has shrunk and whether the pattern of shrinkage is typical of a neurological condition such as Alzheimer's disease. But brain scans are fairly blunt instruments, and the problem is that a significant minority of people who have very poor cognition as measured by psychometric tests have surprisingly normal brain scans. The reverse is also true: some individuals who have no detectable cognitive problems can have scans that show significant brain shrinkage.

We are on firmer ground if we look at individual brain cells under a microscope. Over 100 years ago, Professor Alois Alzheimer himself noted some distinctive characteristics of the brain cells of one of his patients: *amyloid plaques* (clumps of proteins that build up between brain cells) and *neurofibrillary tangles* (twisted strands of protein inside the brain cells themselves).

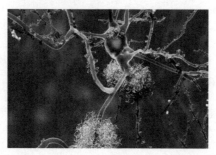

Figure 4 Electron microscope image showing brain cells with amyloid plaques.

Since Alzheimer's original observations, developments in microscope technology have helped scientists to identify and delineate these structures more clearly (see Figure 4), and some progress has been made in understanding how they damage the cell's metabolism. However, there are problems with relying on changes in brain cells to make a diagnosis. First of all, brain cells can only be examined after death (too late), or by carrying out a biopsy of brain tissue in the living patient (too invasive and dangerous).

One way of getting round this is to look for changes in the body, but outside the brain, that might indicate the presence of brain plaques and tangles. There is a lot of research going on to identify these sorts of changes—known as *biomarkers*—in cerebrospinal fluid[6] and in the blood. The hope is to develop a simple and reliable blood test for the presence of brain plaques and tangles. This has not yet been achieved. The persisting problem is that biomarkers in the blood are only indirect measures of changes in the brain and—rather like in a game of Chinese whispers—appear to be approximate and possibly even misleading messengers.

Even if a reliable test for brain plaques and tangles is eventually devised, there remains another key difficulty. In recent years much more data on the brains of the general population has been gathered, and it has become apparent that plaques and tangles are present in the brains of many healthy older people who do not have dementia. It seems that *the connections are not completely tight between the state of an individual's brain, her ability to perform cognitive tests and her lived experience*.

Diagnosis is, therefore, a sophisticated weighing up of the balance of probabilities. An individual attending a dementia clinic will take a series of standardised tests of thinking and memory under the supervision of a psychologist; he and his family will be asked to give a detailed history of the development of his current problems; he may undergo a hands-on examination by a specialist doctor, as well as having blood tests and a brain scan. The results of the tests and examinations are then pieced together to form a picture, but the picture is rather hazy and the diagnosis merely a 'best guess'. For this reason, some would say it is misleading to talk about 'diagnosis' at all. There are other reasons to be at least a little cautious about it. These are well summed up by a phrase coined by researchers Steve Lliffe and Jill Manthorpe: the 'Alzheimerisation of old age'.[7]

The 'Alzheimerisation of old age'?

It is vital to diagnose cancer as early as possible because treatment is more likely to be successful. If the prognosis is poor, at least early diagnosis gives the affected individual and her family time to put things in order, plan terminal care and say their goodbyes. Nowadays, parallels are often drawn between cancer and dementia. In some ways, the parallels are apt. A diagnosis of dementia can prompt the affected individual and her family to make prudent plans for the time when her mental capacity may be lost. Like cancer, dementia has come out of the shadows and is shaking off its stigma; memory clinics are in danger of being swamped by absent-minded middle-aged folk because 'dementia replaced cancer as the nation's greatest fear'.[8]

However, there are some important differences. At the moment, an early diagnosis of dementia does not open the door to treatment and potential cure. In the case of Alzheimer's disease and frontotemporal dementia, medication[9] may be offered, but at best this only alleviates some of the cognitive and behavioural problems rather than slowing or curing the underlying condition, and it can only be taken for a relatively short period of time. The medication can also have significant unwanted side effects (mainly on the digestive system), which have to be weighed against its potential benefits.[10]

Diagnosis may itself bring some unanticipated and unwanted side effects. The affected individual may feel ashamed, and there is some evidence that people withdraw socially and become over-vigilant for signs of cognitive failure. They are also at risk of depression. Those around them (family, healthcare professionals and social care professionals) may become overprotective, and any unusual behaviour may be attributed to the condition rather than to the person. At the level of wider society, it may be more difficult to get travel or driving insurance. There will definitely be a loss of autonomy, and this may be premature in certain areas.

Loss of autonomy is already one of the bugbears of growing older, and once medical language is introduced this process can be intensified and accelerated. Terms like 'sufferer' or 'patient' may be applied to the affected individual. Both these words literally mean 'someone to whom something is done', and they emphasise the loss of autonomy that goes with being assigned a diagnosis. Some more radical analysts have asserted that society has charged healthcare professionals with the task of reducing risk in old age, which has resulted in old age becoming synonymous with disease.[11] This is probably going too far, but it does remind us that the costs of diagnosis need to be balanced against its benefits. Instead of pushing for *early* diagnosis of dementia in all cases, it is better to think in terms of a *timely* diagnosis in *each* case.

But it's good to get medical advice

None of the above should be taken to mean that medical approaches to dementia are a waste of time. *If you are worried about a loved one or suspicious that your own thinking and memory may be failing, you should talk to your family doctor.* This is always the best place to start. It is essential to take very seriously any advice given to you by your general practitioner or other specialist healthcare professional. However, it is also wise to look with a somewhat critical eye, remembering that the issue of diagnosing and treating dementia is more complex than it may at first appear. In particular, you need to reflect on what is best for your individual situation at this particular time, rather than getting sucked into a 'one-size-fits-all' solution.

Dementia is a mysterious condition, and the medical approach of systematically classifying the various forms and distinguishing them from healthy ageing provides some welcome landmarks that help orientate us 'in a strange land'.[12] But if we want to get to know this strange land we will need to go beyond noting the landmarks; we will need to explore it. Our exploration begins in the next chapter by taking a biological approach—finding out more about what is going on in the brains of affected individuals.

Further reading

June Andrews, *Dementia: The one-stop guide* (Profile Books, 2015), chs 1–4.

Notes

1 'Disease' is now considered an outdated medical term. Nowadays doctors more often use the phrase 'health condition', and I follow that convention throughout this book.
2 'Cognition' and 'cognitive function' are more precise terms for the sorts of mental abilities we are talking about in this context—reasoning, memory, perception, language and strategic thinking.

3 Prevalence is the proportion of people living with a condition at any one point in time. (Incidence is the number of new cases per year per head of the population.)

4 *Dementia UK: Second edition—Overview* (Alzheimer's Society, 2014): www.youngdementiauk.org/sites/default/files/Dementia_UK_Second_edition_-_Overview.pdf

5 Pain is underdiagnosed and inadequately treated in people with dementia, and it is the basis of a lot of what gets labelled as 'challenging behaviour'. See, for example, W.P. Achterberg et al., 'Pain management in patients with dementia', *Clinical Interventions in Aging* 8 (2013), pp. 1471–82.

6 Cerebrospinal fluid (CSF) is a colourless liquid that bathes the brain and the spinal cord. It is removed by lumbar puncture, an invasive procedure that is not without risks.

7 S. Lliffe and J. Manthorpe (eds), 'The hazards of early recognition of dementia: a risk assessment', *Aging & Mental Health*, 8 (2004), pp. 99–105.

8 C. Smyth, 'Dementia clinics are swamped by worried well', *The Times* (11 March 2015), p. 1.

9 Donepezil (trade name Aricept®), Galautamine (trade name Reminyl®) and Rivastigmine (trade name Exelon®) are the main ones.

10 Lewy body disease is perhaps an exceptional case here. The extremely distressing nature of some of the symptoms is likely to make the potential benefits of medication outweigh other concerns—see Chapter 2.

11 S.R. Kaufman, 'Old age, disease, and the discourse on risk: geriatric assessment in US health care', *Medical Anthropology Quarterly*, 8 (1994), pp. 430–47.

12 This is the title of an excellent book by Malcolm Goldsmith: *In a Strange Land…: People with dementia and the local church* (4M Publications, 2004).

Chapter 2

A biological approach to dementia: the fading brain

On one occasion in 2015, David Cameron appeared to forget which football team he supports. He actually supports Aston Villa but talked as if he supported West Ham United. In a later interview he aptly named his mysterious mistake a 'brain fade'.[1]

Dementia, like ageing, has a quality of fading. Some people describe the gradual departure of the affected individual as like a series of photocopies of photocopies, which almost imperceptibly move from vivid and vibrant to faded and fragile. And behind the fading of the person is the fading of his brain.

Yet the brain doesn't fade uniformly like a poor photocopy. Neurological conditions affect some parts of the brain more than others—each condition has its own signature pattern of brain fade. Vascular dementia also has its own signature because the physical positioning of the blood vessels means that some parts of the brain are more vulnerable to an interruption of the blood supply than others. In this chapter, we will look at the 'brain-fade signatures' of the main types of dementia, but first we need to familiarise ourselves with the general geography of the brain.

The brain isn't rice pudding—specialisation of function

I once had a friend who said she imagined the brain sat in the skull rather like rice pudding in a tin. Opening the skull to perform brain surgery would then be like opening the tin to reach the homogeneous gelatinous substance inside. This really is a misleading picture. It's more helpful to think in terms of opening a car bonnet to reveal the engine with its various easily recognisable components, all connected to each other and all playing their part in the running of the car, but each with its distinctive identity.

In the last 100 years, there have been massive leaps forward in our understanding of the function of the different parts of the brain. We now know the brain is not a homogeneous mass but a network of highly differentiated parts, each with a very specific function. We might ask why this wasn't obvious to people in earlier centuries (or to my friend). The answer is that our experience of thinking is much more like a continuous whole than a collection of parts or modules, so specialisation of function just didn't feel plausible. Yet we do at times get a glimpse of the individual building blocks of cognition. How often have you remembered everything about a friend except his name? Why, when you can describe him clearly, tell stories about incidents from his life and recall when you last saw him, are you still unable to retrieve his name from your memory? This experience gives us an inkling that our ability to assign names to objects and individuals can work independently of our ability to think about them. A possible reason for this is that the ability to name an individual depends on one brain area, while the ability to know stuff about that individual depends on another brain area.

In fact, it was in the field of language study that the first discoveries of brain specialisation were made. The 19th-century French physician Paul Broca had a patient who was nicknamed 'Tan' because, although he could understand what was said to him, he could only say one word—'Tan'. He had all the equipment necessary for speech—his lips, tongue and vocal cords were perfectly healthy—but he had lost the capacity to express his ideas in words. *He could think in words but not talk in words.* After Tan died, an autopsy showed that he had highly localised damage to an area towards the front of the left half of his brain that has come to be known as 'Broca's area'. Sometime later, the German physician Carl Wernicke was able to identify patients who had the reverse problem. Their speech was fluent, but what they said made no obvious sense and they couldn't understand what was being said to them. *They could talk in words but not think in words.* They had damage somewhat further back in the left half of the brain, an area that unsurprisingly became known as 'Wernicke's area'. These clinical findings were the foundations of what has now become well-established knowledge: the left half of the brain is concerned with language and, even though we experience understanding and expression of language as a continuous whole in our daily conversations, understanding and expression are distinct cognitive processes, and different brain areas specialise in these distinct processes.

Following on from these findings, the whole brain began to be mapped out as the functions of more and more areas were identified. There is still an enormous amount to learn, but we now know a good deal about the specialisations of different centres in the brain and the connections between them.

The brain from top to bottom

It is helpful to think of the brain as being arranged like floors in a department store: the top floors are concerned with high-level cognition, decision making, self-awareness and leisurely reflection; the middle floors are concerned with emotional rapid response to challenge, danger or desire; the lower floors are simply concerned with keeping us alive (see Figure 5). Of course, each of these floors has—as it were—its own rooms and departments. (We might think of Broca's and Wernicke's areas as two separate departments on one of the top floors.)

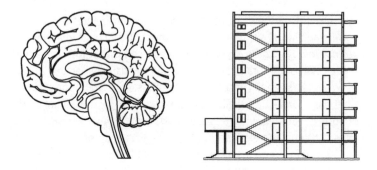

Figure 5 Side-on view of brain; Cross section of a department store.

Translating this into the language of neuroanatomy, and starting at the top, the four main parts of the brain are:

- the cerebral hemispheres
- the limbic system
- the cerebellum
- the brainstem

The top floor: the cerebral hemispheres

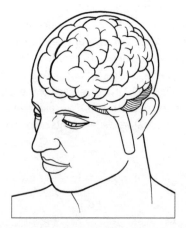

Figure 6 Brain within a human head from the top.

We each have a right and a left cerebral hemisphere, which are mirror images of each other but also physically connected with each other, a bit like the two halves of a walnut (see Figure 6). Each cerebral hemisphere is full of wrinkles and folds. It is like a handkerchief that has been squashed up to fit into a small cup (the skull). If the cerebral hemispheres were unfolded and ironed out, as we might do with the handkerchief, their surface area would be about 2500 cm^2. This very large area means there is room for very complex networks of cells, which can store and process vast amounts of information. The cerebral hemispheres are much more highly developed in humans than in other animals and, as already indicated, are involved with higher cognitive functions such as rational thinking and language. They are divided into a number of lobes (see Figure 7).

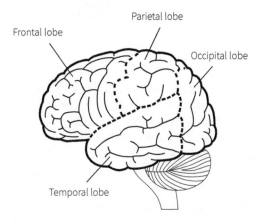

Figure 7   Lobes in the brain.

The middle floor: the limbic system

The limbic system is the name for the collection of centres and circuits that are nestled under the cerebral hemispheres and connected to them. Just as with the cerebral hemispheres, the structures of the limbic system are paired and arranged as mirror images. They are well hidden under the cerebral hemispheres so would only be visible if these were pulled apart to reveal them (that's why you can't see them in the figures above). Figure 8 below shows the limbic system as if revealed through a transparent left cerebral hemisphere.

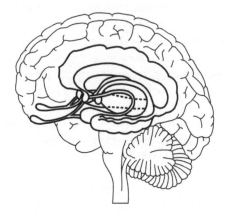

Figure 8 Limbic system.

There are many structures in the limbic system, which is mainly concerned with the processing of emotion. This is not only about feeling emotions, but also about learning to link emotions with other things, for example associating the smell of antiseptic with the feeling of fear. The limbic system is also important in the experience of physical pleasure. Because fear and pleasure are the two basic drivers of behaviour, it follows that the limbic system is important in motivation. Finally, some parts of the limbic system have a vital role in storing and retrieving memories.

The ground floor: the cerebellum

The cerebellum is a convoluted and folded structure, like the cerebral hemispheres but smaller. It is at the base and back of the brain. Again, like the cerebral hemispheres, it has the capacity to process vast amounts of information. However, this is not for higher cognition but for the control of movement through balance and coordination.

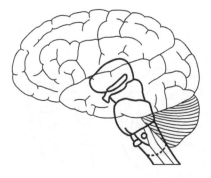

Figure 9 Brainstem.

The basement: the brainstem

The brainstem actually looks like the stem or stalk of a flower, with the rest of the brain sitting on top of it (see Figure 9). It joins the brain to the spinal cord in the neck, and all the messages that pass between brain and body come in and go out through it. On moving from its base to its top, the brainstem gradually gets wider. It is full of little centres responsible for vital functions such as breathing and temperature control, and it is involved in rhythms of sleep and wakefulness. Some key aspects of movement are also controlled by centres which extend upwards from the brainstem into the limbic system. These are called the basal ganglia.

The brain-fade signature of Alzheimer's disease

As we have seen, Alzheimer's disease is characterised by microscopic changes between and inside brain cells (amyloid plaques and neurofibrillary tangles). However, these don't affect the brain uniformly. The problems begin in one specific area in the limbic system, just underneath the temporal lobes of the cerebral hemispheres. This area contains a number of structures that play a crucial part in conscious memory. Probably the most important of these structures are the right hippocampus and left hippocampus (plural: hippocampi). These are so named because early anatomists thought they looked like seahorses, and *hippocampus* is Greek for sea monster (see Figure 10).

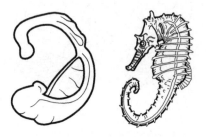

Figure 10 The hippocampus and a seahorse.

The hippocampus acts like an open door that allows two-way traffic: experience passes through it into long-term storage as memories, and the memories that are in storage can be retrieved and pass through it into conscious awareness. When Alzheimer's disease begins, it's as if this door is not fully open; it is harder to get new information in and to get stored information out. As the condition progresses, the door gradually closes until it is firmly shut. This is because brain tissue is dying. On examining the brains of affected individuals in brain scans or post-mortem dissections, it can be seen that the area around the hippocampus has shrunk. This is the brain-fade signature of Alzheimer's disease.

However, as the condition progresses further it affects other parts of the brain. The cerebral hemispheres shrink and higher-order cognition declines. There are also likely to be problems in parts of the brainstem, which may lead to loss of the normal sleep-wake rhythm and also to a general physical restlessness that is usually expressed in the need to pace up and down or walk further afield. What begins as memory loss progresses to problems with all forms of thinking and a general lack of control of basic physical functions.

The brain-fade signature of Lewy body disease

Lewy[2] body disease is named after the particular distinctive microscopic clumps of protein that are found in the brain cells of affected individuals (see Figure 11).

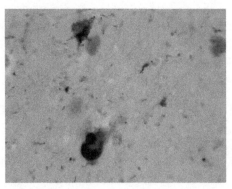

Figure 11 Microscope image of indicators for Lewy body disease.

In many ways Lewy body disease is similar to Alzheimer's disease, but affected individuals show some additional symptoms. The particular brain cells that are affected vary between individuals, and this can make diagnosis difficult. For example, the memory centres in the limbic system are usually affected so this can look very like Alzheimer's disease. It is also very common for the basal ganglia in the brainstem to be affected. These are the structures that go wrong in Parkinson's disease, so Lewy body dementia can also look very like Parkinson's disease: the person may suffer from stiffness, be only able to take little shuffling steps and so on.

One symptom of Lewy body disease that is not usually found in Alzheimer's or Parkinson's is visual hallucinations—seeing things that aren't there. The hallucinations come and go and may also morph into nightmares. They can be extremely distressing, but in some cases they can be alleviated by medication.[3] The hallucinations are thought to arise from changes in the areas of the brain where the limbic system meets the underside of the cerebral hemispheres quite close to the hippocampi.

So, the brain-fade signature of Lewy body disease is more variable than that of Alzheimer's disease, but usually involves the death of brain tissue in the brainstem, limbic system and underside of the temporal lobes of the cerebral hemispheres. Like Alzheimer's disease, the condition progresses so that more widespread areas of the brain gradually become affected.

The brain-fade signature of frontotemporal dementia

While the German psychiatrist Alois Alzheimer was studying the health condition that later bore his name, his Polish contemporary, Arnold Pick, was investigating a progressive neurological condition that was in some respects similar. It also involved a gradual loss of higher cognitive function in affected individuals, but the pattern was different. It tended to have an earlier age of onset—typically in the 50s—and began with disturbing changes in personality rather than memory problems. It had its own distinctive microscopic clumps of proteins (called tau proteins) in the brain cells of affected individuals.

This condition, which seemed to be much rarer than Alzheimer's disease, was known as Pick's disease. Nowadays, it is subsumed into a group of conditions called frontotemporal dementias. They share a common brain-fade signature: the affected areas are the frontal and temporal lobes of the cerebral hemispheres. As with all dementia, the condition eventually progresses so that more widespread areas of the brain become affected.

As their name suggests, the frontal lobes are at the front of the brain. (This may seem obvious but I once had a student who thought they were at the back!) They are far more developed in human beings than in any other mammal, and they are the last area of the brain to become fully functional, not reaching their peak until we are in our late 20s. They are responsible for the planning and implementation of goal-directed behaviour. They keep us on course, helping us to resist distractions; they stop us reacting impulsively and help us to think strategically; they enable us to defer gratification. While we are growing up, our parents or carers act as a kind of proxy set of frontal lobes. They make sure we go to bed early, even when we feel like staying up, because they know how we will feel in the morning; they ensure we do our homework or practice skills, even when this feels like drudgery, reminding us that it'll be worth it in the end; they stop us hurting ourselves by rushing into the road on impulse; and they keep us out of trouble by reminding us that it is rude to speak some thoughts out loud.

As we grow up, we are gradually able to take on these 'executive' functions ourselves because our frontal lobes are maturing. If they are injured or become diseased then we will be in trouble. We may act impulsively or lose our inhibitions, swearing or making personal remarks about other people that would be better left unsaid. We may even behave in a sexually inappropriate way because our usual inhibitions have broken down. We may want our gratification NOW! We may lose empathy for others because we have lost the imagination to see things from any other point of view than our own. We may persist again and again with the same behaviour because we have lost any overall idea of how that individual behaviour connects with the overall task in hand.

A lot of these behaviour patterns can be found in children, but they are mitigated by the charm of youth and by the fact we know they will grow out of them. In a mature adult they can be disastrous: they are very likely to be misunderstood. Other people do not make allowances for individuals with this kind of problem in the way that they might make allowances for someone with memory loss; they simply dislike and judge them. In Chapter 1 we saw that receiving a diagnosis of dementia is not always helpful, but in the case of frontotemporal dementias it nearly always is, because it can at least go some way to reducing this tendency to blame affected individuals for their behaviour.

Because the frontotemporal areas are also involved in language (Broca's area is here), then these dementias may also involve problems with language.

The brain-fade signature of vascular dementia

Dementias that are due to problems with the blood supply to the brain look a bit different from those that are due to brain disease. One difference is in the course of the condition. Instead of an almost imperceptibly gradual decline of cognitive function, vascular dementias proceed in a stepwise fashion as the result of a series of mini-strokes.[4] It's a bit like a house in which the lights go out one by one. One day the lights are on in three rooms. Suddenly the next day the lights are only on in two rooms. The order in which the lights go out depends on which part of the blood supply is being cut off, and this varies a lot from person to person. Typically, a loved one may say something like, 'She was fine yesterday, apart from not knowing where things are in the cupboards, but today she can't speak properly.'

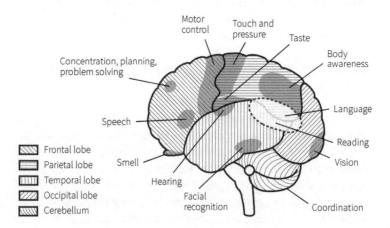

Figure 12 Lobe and cerebellum function.

In vascular dementia, it is often high-level cognitive function that is affected because any part of the cerebral hemispheres can be vulnerable to loss of blood supply. There may be problems with vision or hearing; understanding or expressing language; numerical ability; spatial reasoning (for example, knowing left from right); organising sequences of actions (for example, a relative of mine with vascular dementia became unable to set the table for a meal, something she had been doing automatically since her teenage years); recognising objects (for example, mistaking a comb for a fork or the washbasin for the toilet bowl). (See Figure 12 for the various functions of the cerebral hemispheres.)

Because these problems reveal the fractionated nature of cognition that feels so counterintuitive to us, they can deeply perplex both the affected individual and her loved ones and carers—'How can she name it correctly as a washbasin but still try to pee in it?' As with frontotemporal dementia, the affected person can easily be (mis) judged, this time as showing a kind of wilful stupidity—'He can hear when he wants to hear.'

In this chapter, we have seen that the particular difficulties in cognition, behaviour and emotion that are experienced by people with dementia have their origins in particular types of changes that are taking place in particular parts of their brains. We've also seen how easy it is for these difficulties to be misread by others. This reminds us of the fact that, even though dementia begins in our biology, it is a highly social condition that is lived out in relationships. The next chapter pursues social approaches to dementia, looking at how on the one hand society shapes and defines dementia, and how on the other hand dementia impacts on social relationships.

Further reading

Oliver Sacks, *The Man Who Mistook His Wife for a Hat* (Picador, 2011).

Notes

1 He borrowed this expression from another politician, Natalie Bennett, who had gone to pieces during a BBC radio interview.
2 German neurologist Dr Friedrich Heinrich Lewy (1885–1950) discovered these clumps of protein.
3 There is some evidence that Donepezil and Rivastigmine are effective in reducing hallucinations in people with Lewy body disease.
4 This is not the same as a transient ischemic attack (TIA), which is also sometimes referred to as a mini-stroke. As its name indicates, a TIA is a short-lived event whose effects are not permanent. However, both TIAs and vascular dementia are signs that all is not well with the cardiovascular system.

Chapter 3

A social approach to dementia: not gone but forgotten

Towards the end of their lives my parents, neither of whom had dementia, moved into sheltered accommodation. The development was very pleasant with lovely gardens and good care support. Nevertheless, my father insisted on calling their apartment 'the *oubliette*',[1] a reference to the chambers in castles like the Bastille, where prisoners were placed out of sight and so out of mind. In the same vein, it has been said that the tragedy in dementia is not so much that individuals forget as that they are forgotten.

There is a very real sense in which society would like to forget people with dementia. This is not so much out of cruelty or callousness but because the existence of people with dementia reminds us of things we would rather forget. One way of forgetting people with dementia is to try to turn them into people without dementia—to pay a lot of attention to finding a cure. At the Dementia Summit in 2013, the G8 nations committed themselves to finding a cure or an effective treatment by 2025, with the UK aiming to double its annual research funding to reach £132 million by then. The year 2025 is, of course, about the time when people from the baby boomer generation like me will start worrying about the possibility of getting dementia. If we can find a cure, or believe that one is just around the corner, then our lives will look less uncertain and frightening. But, if it turns out that there is little prospect of a silver bullet that will dispense with dementia once and for all, we will continue to be disquieted by the presence of older people with dementia who confront us with the fact that not everything in life can be fixed by ingenuity, effort and money.

Dead or alive?

Yet there is more to this than our collective need to convince ourselves that we can control our own futures. There is something about the nature of dementia itself that frightens us. People in the advanced stages of dementia are in a strange limbo state: they are clearly alive, yet in another sense they seem to have departed, to have died. They therefore confront us with our own mortality in a way that is much more disturbing than attending a funeral or seeing the body of a deceased person. Dementia has often (unfortunately) been described as a 'living death', and it is a very small step from this description to the idea of the 'undead' or zombie.

Zombies are beings found in the mythology of many cultures, always evoking fear and loathing. They are deeply ambiguous—neither fish nor fowl—and ambiguity makes us uneasy to say the least. What's more, most zombie myths include the idea that if the zombie gets you, you too will become one of the undead. This is vividly exemplified in the Dementors of the Harry Potter books—soulless creatures who suck the souls from their victims.

American political scientist Susan Behuniak has investigated popular and scholarly literature on Alzheimer's disease and has come to the conclusion that, in the English-speaking world at least, people with dementia are not too far removed from zombies in the public imagination. Behuniak argues convincingly that 'strong negative emotional responses to AD are… buttressed by the social construction of people with AD as zombies… it infuses the social discourse about AD with a politics of revulsion and fear that separates and marginalises those with AD.'[2]

This is an important insight because it shows up the unconscious primitive psychological forces that underlie our supposedly civilised and enlightened attitudes to dementia. Very few of us would say that people with advanced dementia are like zombies; indeed, we are likely to find the idea offensive. But our emotional response to them may tell a different story, and this response is usually a desire to keep our distance.

The zombie myth pervades many cultures, but there is also a quintessentially English idea that is also unconsciously applied to people with dementia. This is the 'nutter in the attic' motif, perhaps originating from the character of Mrs Rochester in Charlotte Brontë's novel *Jane Eyre*, a deranged and dangerous creature kept under lock and key out of sight at the top of the house, from where she occasionally escapes.

Many residential care homes for older people have more than one floor and, where they do, it is those with dementia-related challenging behaviour who are housed at the top. Their desire is to get out into the world beyond the walls that confine them, but this is made very difficult because they will need to negotiate stairs or operate a lift if they are to have any chance of reaching an external door. Not infrequently, residents who have been easy to manage on admission to a care home are moved upstairs when their behaviour becomes more challenging. The expectation is that they will not be coming back down again in this life. Of course, this arrangement has the residents' best interests at heart; the staff must exercise their duty of care and minimise undue risk. But we would do well to pause and reflect on the symbolism conveyed by this habit of placing the most disturbed and disturbing individuals upstairs, out of sight and hearing, behind many barriers.

It takes two (or more) to make dementia

Susan Behuniak uses the phrase 'social construction' in the quote above. What she means by this is that the brain changes that happen to people with dementia are only part of their condition. Dementia is 'constructed' through the interplay between the biological state of the individual and the way other people think about and treat him, which in turn affects how he thinks about and treats himself.

The concept of 'teenager' is a good analogy here. Of course, young people undergo significant biological changes around the time of puberty, but the description of young people as teenagers is a very recent development dating from the years after World War II and driven by the agendas of big commercial companies. They spotted a promising gap in the market and a group who might, either indirectly through pressure on parents, or through their own spending power, make a good marketing target. Nowadays, we don't often question the reality of being a teenager, with all its connotations of rebellion, and the embracing of certain sorts of clothing, music and peer group norms. But it's a social construction as much as a biological condition, and one in which money has always played a big part.

Money is also an important aspect of dementia. The pharmaceutical companies that invest so heavily in research and development of medications for dementia have their own financial agenda. This is not to suggest they are in any way corrupt, but they do influence the way that dementia is thought and talked about (as an illness to be treated with their medications). As we've seen, governments too can affect the way we think about dementia by how far up the spending priority list they place it, and by the aspect of dementia care they choose to target (developing new medications, or increasing care workers' wages, or improving residential accommodation, or developing community projects and so on).

More obviously, dementia has very significant direct financial cost implications for people with the diagnosis, together with any dependants or beneficiaries they may have. A diagnosis of dementia often brings with it a prognosis of poverty. When my father was told he had terminal cancer, he said he was pleased because at least he didn't have dementia. He explained that this was not so much because of a dread of declining cognition, but a fear that his modest yet hard-earned financial assets would be stripped from him by the costs of care. He spent his last weeks in a hospice, free of charge, deeply satisfied in the knowledge that he would be able to leave his life savings to his family.

In Part 2 we will look in detail at how dementia can strip a person of his or her identity. Here it is worth pausing to consider that my father was a bank manager. His desire to hold on to his assets and manage them responsibly was not about personal greed; *it was an essential part of who he was*. He had, after all, done this for others for the whole of his working life. What's more, he correctly saw that this aspect of his identity could be destroyed not by the biology of dementia, but by the way society treats people with this diagnosis.

If we go back to the introductory exercise on page 11, we can see that most of the things that characterise people with dementia are to do with their social condition, and much of this is connected with stigma. The two main issues are funding of services for people with dementia (as my father was only too aware) and exclusion from community life.

Healthcare or social care?

While there is general agreement that dementia arises from recognised health conditions (for example, Alzheimer's disease), being diagnosed with such a condition does not guarantee access to NHS-funded care. This is because the needs of most people affected by dementia are deemed to be social rather than health related.[3] This may seem illogical, but the question in the mind of the funding authorities is not so much what is causing the person's situation as what kind of assistance he or she requires and from whom. If the person requires regular injections, these must be administered by a qualified healthcare professional, so this is deemed a healthcare need. On the other hand, if the person requires assistance with getting dressed, or making a meal, or taking tablets, this could be undertaken by a medically unqualified care assistant, so this is deemed a social or personal care need.

The crucial point is that healthcare is provided by the NHS, which is free at the point of delivery (whether in hospital or the community), but social and personal care is provided by the local government authority, and most recipients pay for all or part of it depending on their income, amount of savings and other assets. This is true whether the social or personal care is provided in the person's own home or in a residential institution. Because contributions are means-tested, people who are already feeling vulnerable or even ashamed have to expose their previously private financial affairs to the scrutiny of local authorities. Many find this a deeply intrusive experience, and some decide to pay for all their care themselves in order to avoid it.

We might want to argue that some needs arising directly from the health condition, for example, the psychological need to participate in reminiscence sessions, are best met by a qualified healthcare professional such as a nurse, occupational therapist or psychologist. However, as these sorts of interventions are not subject to strict legal regulation and could (allegedly) be delivered in some form by medically unqualified carers or volunteers, such arguments remain academic, especially in a climate where money is short and funding of public services is being squeezed. A basic rule of thumb is that health needs are those that require *specialist* administration of *physical* treatments;[4] the emphasis is on the body rather than the mind.

In 2011 the government-commissioned, independent Dilnot Report found that 'The current adult social care funding system in England is not fit for purpose and needs urgent and lasting reform,' and that 'A major problem is that people are unable to protect themselves against very high care costs... There is great uncertainty and people are worried about the future.'[5] This is, of course, particularly true for people affected by dementia. In response, the government introduced the Care Act of 2014[6] (affecting England and Wales), which was implemented in part in April 2015 and will be implemented in full in April 2020. Its aims are to protect people from 'catastrophic care costs' by introducing a cap of £72,000 on their total contributions, and to protect people with 'modest wealth' by offering some degree of financial help towards the costs of personal or social care to those whose total assets are around £118,000 or less.

This will obviously be a significant improvement on the current situation, where there is no cap on the total contributions required of an individual, and financial help is only available to people whose total assets are around £23,000 or less (hence the sad stories of people having to sell their family homes to meet care bills). However, it remains the case that the personal financial costs of dementia-related health conditions are significantly greater than, for example, for most cancers. Rightly or wrongly, as a society we have chosen to make life-saving or life-prolonging medication, surgery and other treatments free, but to charge individuals for life-giving practical and emotional care.

Outside the camp

The vast majority of people with dementia who need care, whether it be continuing healthcare, or social and personal care, would strongly prefer to receive this in their own homes. However, about one third of these are in residential care homes, and this in turn makes them more likely to be admitted to hospital.[7] At any one time about a quarter of hospital beds in England are occupied by people with dementia.[8]

For many people with advanced dementia, residential care is the only realistic available option. However, there is evidence that individuals are often admitted to hospital unnecessarily or placed in residential care too early, either because sufficient appropriate home care is not readily available or because there has been little in the way of advance planning so that a crisis leads to panic on the part of loved ones or professionals.

People who are in residential care or hospital have effectively been removed from community life. They cease to function as citizens in the public square. They are seen no more and easily forgotten. Of course, some care homes make great efforts to connect with their local communities, but this is not always easy to deliver, especially for residents with dementia, and many care homes don't even try. People with dementia who do remain in their own homes have a better chance of being connected with and participating actively in their local communities, but there are still some major obstacles to overcome.

The obstacles can be practical or have more to do with the closed-minded attitudes of others, but increasingly they have come to be understood as symptoms of a *political* issue—the place of people with dementia in society as a whole. This has been helped along by thinking of dementia as a disability rather than an illness. Disabled people fall under the scope of national and European equality and human rights legislation. They have 'disability rights'. People with dementia have disabilities so why shouldn't they benefit from this too? The phrase 'dementia rights' is starting to appear in public discourse.[9]

In 2012, then Prime Minister David Cameron issued his 'challenge on dementia', a strategic programme involving increased government funding not only for primary medical research but also to support people in living well with dementia. In this context, the idea of the 'dementia-friendly *community*' was born.[10] Accordingly, when the second phase of the challenge on dementia was launched in 2015, Cameron emphasised the vital role of communities: 'As we look to the future, it is clear that we all have a part to play. This is not just about funding from government, or research by scientists, but understanding and compassion from all of us.'[11]

The Alzheimer's Society has a formal recognition process for dementia-friendly communities, which is widely used. Under this system a dementia-friendly community is one that:

- shapes itself around the views of people with dementia and their carers.
- promotes and maintains independence for people living with dementia by delivering community-based solutions.
- challenges stigma and builds awareness about dementia.
- supports people with dementia to engage in community life.
- ensures that community activities include people with dementia.
- empowers people with dementia and recognises their contribution.

For any given community (town, business, public service, hospital, etc.) this is achieved through dementia-awareness training, addressing transport needs, improved signage, the setting up of groups that champion the interests of people with dementia and so on. Befriending programmes are often a key component of this approach because it is not enough that people with dementia engage in their communities; like all of us, they need to feel part of a network of relationships.

Loneliness and dementia

Loneliness is an increasingly recognised issue in our society. Feelings of loneliness are a normal part of our experience. Like hunger, thirst and pain, they tell us we need something—in this case, contact with people.

It is helpful to think about contact with people as providing something deeper. Just as good food provides something deeper—energy and material to build and repair our bodies—good contact with people provides social stimulation, a sense of belonging and intimacy. Just as we need a well-balanced diet to flourish physically, we need social stimulation, belonging and intimacy if we are to flourish psychologically. When these needs are met, our sense of loneliness disappears. Yet for many the feeling of loneliness persists and becomes a chronic problem because their need cannot be met. Research indicates that about 6% of the population describe themselves as feeling lonely most or all of the time, but this figure is a bit misleading because it is an average. Rates of loneliness are very low in young adulthood and middle age, but higher in the youngest adults under 25 who have not yet found a life partner, and in older adults over 55 who are retiring, losing partners and whose children are moving away. Loneliness is highest in adults over 75, about 12% of whom report feeling lonely most or all of the time, and it appears to affect women more than men.[12]

These days, children tend to move away from their family of origin. This means that ageing parents are often far apart from their adult children and grandchildren. Sometimes they move (or worse 'are moved') to be closer to their adult offspring. This often uproots them from a place that holds deep memories, valued roles and social networks, and they are not always able to establish new social networks before they become frail. This is profoundly alienating for many. Sometimes the reason for the move is the family's concern that an older person's cognition is failing. So just at the point when familiar anchors in her surroundings are crucial, she is cut loose from them.

An older person can be the 'last one standing' from their generation of family and friends. The loneliness this evokes is existential: when there is nobody left to remember who you once were, 'nobody left who knows what I am talking about' (as an older friend once said to me), then you are profoundly less yourself. Even if an older person has a good number of social contacts, there may still be a lack of the intimacy that can only be provided by someone who has known you well over many years.

Loneliness is associated with poor mental and physical health. While depression leads to loneliness, loneliness also leads to depression, and there is increasing evidence that loneliness has direct effects on hormones and the immune system.[13] There is thus a vicious circle at work.

The same is true for dementia. While it is obvious that dementia can make people socially isolated,[14] it is also true that social isolation can make dementia worse. Research has found that people with Alzheimer's disease show fewer cognitive problems on testing if their social networks are rich: that is, two individuals who have suffered identical brain changes may show quite different levels of symptoms depending on the degree and quality of their contact with other people.[15] In Chapter 1 we saw that 'the connections are not completely tight between the state of an individual's brain, her ability to perform cognitive tests and her lived experience'. It seems that reducing loneliness is one of the things that can loosen these connections to good effect. If this is true, *befriending people with dementia is not just a compassionate act of inclusion and solidarity; it may actually impact directly on their cognitive abilities.*

Who is 'affected by dementia'?

The effects of dementia go beyond the person who is diagnosed with the condition. We might think of dementia as something that spreads out and affects all who are in relationship with him. We might say there is one person 'with dementia' but a whole group of people 'affected by dementia'. We might go further and say that the core problem in dementia is not so much damaged brain cells as damaged relationships.

The strain on the nearest and dearest of the person with dementia is enormous and changes over time. In the early stages, there may be an attempt to cover up the condition, to shield a spouse or parent from embarrassment. Then there may be a phase of persuading him to seek medical help and to give up control in key aspects of his life such as finances or driving. There may well be financial worries as discussed earlier in this chapter, and the challenge of giving care or organising others to give care. If the individual goes into a residential facility, there is likely to be guilt. Meanwhile, a beloved parent, spouse or partner is gradually departing—yet there may be little time or opportunity to make sense of this, or to grieve, because the practicalities of life are so pressing.

Different people are affected differently by all of this, and much depends on the quality of the pre-existing relationships. However, the children of a person with dementia often seem to take it particularly hard. Part of the reason may be the role reversal that can take place: there is pain for both the person with dementia and his or her children in accepting that the one who, for so many years, has been the adult carer is now a childlike recipient of care. More profoundly, we get our earliest sense of being a real person in the world as we gaze into the eyes of a loving parent. It is almost as if the intimate parental gaze of love, knowledge and hope actually creates us. When that gaze becomes dimmed or vacant, we may feel that we have not only lost our parent but also lost something of ourselves.

This perhaps explains the intense distress experienced by the children of people with dementia and their sometimes unhelpful attempts to manage it. Some people push their parents too hard—'Come *on* Mum, you can remember if you try!' Others distance themselves either physically or, more commonly, emotionally, getting involved in the practical aspects of care but avoiding any real engagement with the parent who seems to be departing. Most common of all is the continued questioning of self and others—'Even though she doesn't seem to recognise me, is there perhaps a spark in there of remembrance and love for me?'

It is not just the person with dementia who is lonely and lost.

There are circles of impact on close relatives and carers, professional carers, friends and extended family, including grandchildren, and the wider society of whom the affected individual is a part. Any approach to the spiritual care of 'those affected by dementia' needs to take this into account. Yet at the centre of this circle is the *person* with dementia. We have now completed our overview of the different ways of thinking about dementia as a 'condition', and in Part 2 we start to focus on this person at the centre.

Further reading

Alexine Crawford, *The Challenge of Caring: Bible-based reflections* (BRF, 2011).
June Andrews, *Dementia: The one-stop guide* (Profile Books, 2015), Chapters 10–11.
For a dementia services directory see www.alzheimers.org.uk/local-information/dementia-connect/#!/search
Safeguarding the Convoy: A call to action from the Campaign to End Loneliness (Campaign to End Loneliness and Age UK Oxfordshire,

2011): www.campaigntoendloneliness.org/wp-content/uploads/downloads/2011/07/safeguarding-the-convey_-_a-call-to-action-from-the-campaign-to-end-loneliness.pdf

Jo Ind, *Loneliness: Accident or injustice? Exploring Christian Responses to Loneliness in the Thames Valley* (The Archway Foundation and the Diocese of Oxford, 2016): www.oxford.anglican.org/wp-content/uploads/2013/01/OD701-loneliness-book.pdf

Notes

1 From the French *oublier*—to forget.

2 S.M. Behuniak, 'The living dead? The construction of people with Alzheimer's disease as zombies', *Ageing & Society,* 31 (2011), pp. 70–92.

3 This can and often should be challenged on a case-by-case basis. For a useful guide on how to do this, and the broader issues involved, see *When Does the NHS Pay for Care? How to apply for NHS continuing healthcare in England and how to appeal if it is not awarded* (Alzheimer's Society, 2016): www.alzheimers.org.uk/site/scripts/download_info.php?fileID=75

4 Or occasionally specialist administration of psychological treatments for *physically* risky symptoms such as intense restlessness or aggressive outbursts.

5 Commission on Funding of Care and Support, *Fairer Care Funding: The report of the Commission on Funding of Care and Support* (2011), p. 5.

6 www.legislation.gov.uk/ukpga/2014/23/contents

7 *Support. Stay. Save: Care and support of people with dementia in their own homes* (Alzheimer's Society, 2011): www.alzheimers.org.uk/site/scripts/download_info.php?fileID=1030

8 Department of Health, *Dementia: A state of the nation report on dementia care and support in England* (Williams Lea, 2013): www.gov.uk/government/uploads/system/uploads/attachment_data/file/262139/Dementia.pdf

9 G. McGettrick, *Dementia, Rights, and the Social Model of Disability: A new direction for policy and practice?* (Mental Health Foundation, 2015): www.mentalhealth.org.uk/sites/default/files/dementia-rights-policy-discussion.pdf

10 G. Green and L. Lakey, *Building Dementia-Friendly Communities: A priority for everyone* (Alzheimer's Society, 2013): www.alzheimers.org.uk/site/scripts/download_info.php?fileID=1916

11 Department of Health, *Prime Minister's Challenge on Dementia 2020*

(Williams Lea, 2015), p. 3: www.gov.uk/government/uploads/system/uploads/attachment_data/file/414344/pm-dementia2020.pdf

12 C.R. Victor and K. Yang, 'The prevalence of loneliness among adults: a case study of the United Kingdom', *The Journal of Psychology: Interdisciplinary and Applied* 146 (2012), pp. 85–104.

13 L. Hawkley and J.T. Cacioppo, 'Loneliness matters: a theoretical and empirical review of consequences and mechanisms', *Annals of Behavioural Medicine,* 40 (2010), pp. 218–27.

14 M. Kane and L. Cook, *Dementia 2013: The hidden voice of loneliness* (Alzheimer's Society, 2013): www.alzheimers.org.uk/site/scripts/download_info.php?fileID=1677

15 D.A. Bennett et al., 'The effect of social networks on the relation between Alzheimer's disease pathology and level of cognitive function in old people: a longitudinal cohort study', *The Lancet: Neurology,* 5 (2006), pp. 406–12.

Part 2

Thinking about the person with dementia

Dementia throws up all sorts of questions about what it means to be a human being. It confronts us with the fact that we are materially embodied and deeply fragile creatures. It presents us with the mystery that some microscopic physical changes in our brains seem to have the capacity, like the well-named Dementors in 'Harry Potter', to rob us of our very souls.

A quarter of a century ago, the American neuropsychologist George Prigatano wrote an article in which he reflected on the way that brain disease and injury not only affect the individual's capacity to perform tasks, but have a much deeper personal impact. The title of his paper was 'Disordered mind, wounded soul'.[1]

This talk of souls invites us to think a bit more deeply about what we mean when we use that word. I would suggest that, in everyday conversation, the word 'soul' is used in two senses that are often combined with each other: first to mean the 'essential me' (as in Bob Dylan's famous line 'I gave her my heart but she wanted my soul'[2]); secondly to mean the seat of my capacity for some sort of spiritual life—what the New Testament calls my 'spirit'. We shall see that both soul and spirit can be deeply affected by dementia.

In the next three chapters we will look into this further, considering the impact of dementia on conscious reflective thinking and memory in Chapter 4, and how dementia leads to an unravelling of personality in Chapter 5. In Chapter 6 the wisdom of the Christian tradition is brought to bear on the issue of dementia's apparent capacity to steal away our souls, and we find that it offers a different and more hopeful perspective. To anticipate the conclusion of Part 2 and to paraphrase the apostle Paul: 'I am convinced that neither death, nor life, nor angels, nor rulers, nor things present, nor things to come, nor powers, nor height, nor depth, nor anything else in all creation—not even dementia—will be able to separate us from the love of God in Christ Jesus our Lord' (Romans 8:38–39, altered).

Notes

1 G. Prigatano, 'Disordered mind, wounded soul: the emerging role of psychotherapy in rehabilitation after brain injury', *Journal of Head Trauma Rehabilitation,* 6 (1991), pp. 1–10.

2 Bob Dylan, 'Don't think twice, it's all right' (copyright © Warner Brothers, 1963).

Chapter 4

I think therefore I am?

As mind and memory long since said goodbye,
'I think therefore I am' does not apply.
But there are days when I take heart because
I think I thought therefore perhaps I was.

This anonymous poem entitled 'After Descartes' gives a wry take on the French philosopher's famous statement *'Cogito ergo sum'*—the idea that I know I exist because I am engaged in the activity of thinking.[1] The statement contains within it two key values that have continued to be characteristic of Western society up until this day: the emphasis on the *individual*—'I' rather than 'we'—and the very high status given to *rational thought*. According to Descartes (and many who have come after him), conscious reflective thought isn't just desirable—it's essential to our very being.

The poem, written from the perspective of an older person whose cognition is failing, raises the disquieting consequence of Descartes' assertion. If thinking is essential to existence, then if I can't think (properly) it follows that I don't exist as a recognisable individual. As the poem indicates, if I am to think properly I need memory. So it follows that 'I think therefore I am' entails *I remember therefore I am*.

This does make some sense. We each have our story. Individuals and communities build and maintain their identities through the construction and repetition of stories, punctuated by 'self-defining memories'.[2] We recall our first day at school, the first time we read *The Catcher in the Rye*, our first taste of champagne, the time our world was turned upside down by a new insight or encounter. These sorts of events and experiences are woven together to make us who we are and, as we repeat the story to ourselves and others, our identity becomes more fully embedded. Religious and civic rituals such as the Jewish festival of Passover and Remembrance Day on 11 November bind communities together in a common story that is received and passed on in actions that say, 'This is who we are!' If we forget our story, we are in great danger of losing ourselves.

As we have seen, not all types of dementia are dominated by memory problems. Nevertheless, the majority are; the affected individuals forget their own stories and as a result their souls can seem diminished or even wounded. In order to understand how this forgetting comes about, we need to know a bit more about how memory works and how it goes wrong in dementia.

Memories are made of this

There are several different sorts of memory. There seem to be different sorts of memory for different sorts of material (for example recognising faces as opposed to recalling names), and different sorts of memory for different periods in our life. We hear talk of 'long-term and short-term memory', 'emotional memory', 'bodily memory' and so on.

Psychologists who specialise in the study of memory divide it into many categories. We will begin by looking at two of the most important: 'working memory' and 'long-term memory'.

Working memory

Working memory is basically what we can hold in our attention at any one time while we are thinking. If a friend tells you a telephone number and you don't have a means of recording it to hand, you will have to repeat it to yourself (preferably out loud) and avoid any distractions from anything else until you can get to your notepad or enter it into your mobile phone. By doing this you are keeping it 'live' in your working memory. If you do get distracted en route you will lose the telephone number permanently. However, if you were to rehearse it for long enough, you would find that you had retained it (this is what goes on in rote learning). So, while some information just passes through our working memory and gets lost ('in one ear and out the other'), other information passes from our working memory into our longer-term storage.

Long-term memory

Long-term memory is our memory store for everything we have learnt from our early years up until the present. Many people use the phrase 'long-term memory' to mean memory for long ago, but the technical term for this is actually remote memory. This is an example of a difference between the language of the general public and the language of professional experts—it can be quite confusing. Therefore, this book avoids the phrase 'long-term memory' altogether and instead focuses on its two main components, explicit memory[3] and implicit memory, looking first at explicit memory in this chapter and then at implicit memory in Chapter 5.

Explicit memory refers to the sorts of memories that you know you know. For example, if I asked you what your mother's name was, you would most likely know the answer and you would know that you know the answer. Explicit memory is itself generally divided into memory for facts[4] (for example, the name of your mother), and memory for events[5] (for example, that you visited your mother last weekend).

Storing and retrieving explicit memories: the airing cupboard analogy

In Alzheimer's and related conditions, working memory remains relatively intact but explicit memory is gradually and relentlessly eroded. The airing cupboard is perhaps the best picture of the way that explicit memory goes wrong in these conditions. Like all analogies, it has its limits and shouldn't be pressed too far; it is nevertheless illuminating.

Imagine for a moment that you are a newly-wed, proud of your wedding gifts, among which is a quantity of household linen. You place it, carefully ironed and scattered with sprigs of lavender and rose petals, on the bottom shelf of your airing cupboard. Over the years, with the realities of family life, easy-care sheets get chucked in on top, unironed, unsprinkled and without much thought to order. Then, as life becomes more and more demanding, a whole assortment of socks and underpants are bunged in on the very top in a totally chaotic arrangement.

While you can open the door of the cupboard, it is fairly easy to reach in and find the item you want. But what if the door starts gradually to close? (Recall from Chapter 2 that as the hippocampus starts to shrink and die it is rather like a door closing.) You have to reach in through a narrowing gap and feel about for what you want. It will be easier then to find and identify the linen you laid down when you were a fresh and naively optimistic young newly-wed. If you do stumble on that sock you wanted, it will be due more to luck than strategy.

Something like this is going on when we retrieve memories from storage. The ones that have been laid down the longest are the most deeply embedded in an orderly fashion. They have had time to be consolidated. This is one reason that, as the memory of people with dementia starts to decline, it is the most recent memories that are the most difficult for them to retrieve and the memories from long ago that seem most vivid to them. Of course, there will also be emotional reasons for this—it's pleasant to live in the past if the current reality is one of disorientation and decline—but the main reason for the tendency to remember the distant past more readily than the present is inherent to the way memory works.

Finally, the door shuts. You are then pretty stuck. Not only can you no longer get stuff out of the airing cupboard, you can't put any new stuff in. In terms of memory, you are not able to remember *any* facts or events—old or new—any more. But then you notice there are some cracks and a couple of knotholes in the door, and a loose piece of wood in the side of the cupboard. You get glimpses of what is inside, and with care may even be able to retrieve the odd small item. You don't have any choice about what you get; it's simply what happens to be adjacent to the cracks.

This is a way of understanding what is going on when people who have apparently lost all memories have random 'lucid moments'. These can be deeply moving for loved ones but they are not a sign that the door will open again. Sometimes they seem to happen spontaneously. Sometimes they come in response to the psychological equivalent of reaching into a crack—approaching the memory obliquely rather than directly, for example through music, scent or touch.

We need to bear in mind one important caveat about the airing cupboard analogy: memories are not stored fully formed in the brain like items in a cupboard. It is more that the process of retrieval itself 'makes' the memory. So we can't simply do the psychological equivalent of breaking the door down to get at the trapped memories. But precisely because the airing cupboard analogy gives such a good picture of what it can be like to live with someone whose memory is failing, we can find ourselves pressing it too far. We batter at the cupboard door by asking repeated direct questions of the one who is slipping away from us and urging him to try harder; we attempt to prise the door open by giving him clues in the hope that they will jog his memory; meanwhile, we are looking everywhere for the magic key that will unlock the door once and for all.

These things are natural and a measure of our grief, but they don't help anyone. That battering against the door is an emotional battering of the affected person because asking a direct question of an individual with dementia invites failure, and with it shame or anxiety. Those attempts to prise the door open are futile and intrusive; when a lucid moment comes we can only accept it with joy as a one-off gift—a glimpse through a crack—and we need to resist the temptation to read too much into it. Above all, there is no magic key that will restore what has been lost.

'The person I miss most is me'[6]

And what exactly has been lost? The gradual fading of explicit memory for the past means that I can no longer say where I come from, both in concrete terms and in a more metaphorical sense. The life experience and wisdom that I have accrued, the interweaving of my story with the stories of others, is also lost to me, and with it the basis of our relationships. One of the great pleasures of later life is reminiscing with old friends. This often results in laughter that is a mystery to those who do not share their set of experiences; 'You have to have been there!' we explain. As we lose our life story, we lose the capacity to 'be there' again, to participate in that wider story.

In a more immediate sense, if I can't tell you what I did today, or recall what you said to me yesterday, our conversation will soon peter out and our relationship become frustrating and impoverished. Family life is held together by 'What kind of day have you had?', 'You should hear the day I've had!', 'You'll never guess who I saw today…' and so on.

Being in the present is also a profoundly different experience because it no longer provides the building blocks for a narrative of my life but is simply experienced in the moment, rather like a telephone number that I never get to write down. Making decisions about future courses of action also becomes impossible because they depend so heavily on having good information about the present and the past. Those of us who are ageing will know the feeling of going into a room with a purpose and then forgetting why we went there. In dementia, all purposeful activity can feel like that. If I can't recall my wider context as a storied being who is part of a storied community, I will become like a small child—only able to act in the very short term or react to my immediate circumstances.

As my memory systems unravel, my identity as an individual person and social being also unravels. At some point, I will probably be unable even to recall my own name.

Memory and transcendence

In the Greek New Testament, the word that is most often used to refer to identity is *psuchē* (from which we get 'psychology'). This word has traditionally been translated into English as 'soul'. In modern Bibles *psuchē* is sometimes translated 'soul' (Luke 1:46), but also 'life' (Matthew 6:25), 'self' (Luke 12:19 NIV), 'person' (Romans 13:1) or simply 'me' (Matthew 26:38), depending on the context. This range of words give a good sense of the actual meaning of *psuchē*. From this we see that basically I don't have a soul; I *am* my soul.

The New Testament understanding of the human person also involves another aspect, *pneuma*, usually translated 'spirit' or 'breath'. *Pneuma* and *psuchē* are closely connected. Mary expresses this close connection when she says, 'My soul magnifies the Lord, and my spirit rejoices in God my Saviour' (Luke 1:46–47). But they do have distinct meanings. *Pneuma* can mean simple physical life denoted by breathing, but it also has a more significant theological meaning, referring to life in relation to the things of God, or the 'spiritual life'.

In our increasingly secular society, the idea of spirituality has become rather dislocated from religion. Indeed, these days many people describe themselves as 'spiritual but not religious'.[7] This might be troubling to Christians, but it does mean that we have a link into the secular world via the concept of 'spirituality'. Human spirituality is a sign that we are made in the image of God; in it, we can see the yearnings of human souls for the maker they do not fully know. This yearning is recognised by the apostle Paul in his moving speech to the Athenians:

> 'Athenians, I see how extremely religious [we might say 'spiritual'] you are in every way. For as I went through the city and looked carefully at the objects of your worship, I found among them an altar with the inscription, "To an unknown god". What therefore you worship as unknown, this I proclaim to you… From one ancestor he made all nations to inhabit the whole earth, and he

allotted the times of their existence and the boundaries of the places where they would live, so that they would search for God and perhaps grope for him and find him—though indeed he is not far from each one of us. For "In him we live and move and have our being."'

ACTS 17:22B–23, 26–28A

Human spirituality has been described as the making of meaning through the practice of transcendence. People make meaning by engaging with big questions about the purpose of life and their place in it, including questions like, 'What does it mean to be human?' and 'Who am I?' As they do this they may, to use Paul's words, search and grope for something beyond themselves; they practice transcendence.

The Oxford English Dictionary defines transcendence as 'existence or experience beyond the normal or physical level'. It's got something to do with stretching ourselves so that we reach or are moved into another place. This may be a move outwards towards others, inwards into the self or upwards towards 'something higher':

1 Transcendence of self-absorption by *going beyond* self-centred concerns and forming genuine relationships with others so that our purpose in life is broadened.
2 Transcendence of mundane experience by *entering into* altered states of consciousness (perhaps through prayer or meditation) that may support new insights into meaning.
3 Transcendence of the immediate situation by *rising above* it and engaging with a 'higher' or 'ultimate' perspective.

These ideas about transcendence become important as we struggle with the question of how to support the spiritual lives of all people, regardless of whether they espouse any kind of formal religious faith. We will explore the practicalities of this in Part 3. First, we need to recognise that dementia can impair my ability to transcend and, in so doing, rob me of my spirituality. In other words, dementia can threaten not only my soul—who I am (my *psuchē*)—but also my spirit—my potential for relationship with God (my *pneuma*).

The church father Augustine of Hippo (AD354–430) had a great interest in what we would now call psychology, and he devoted a whole chapter of his *Confessions* (Book 10) to memory and its theological implications. Commenting on this, Rowan Williams notes that Augustine went so far as to identify memory with spirit because:

> Memory… is my presence to myself, the way in which I constitute myself and understand myself as a subject with a continuous history of experience. I am not trapped and confined in the present moment: as a conscious subject with a remembered past, I *'transcend'* these limitations. I can understand them, put them in perspective, move on from and through them. Thus whatever stimulates and nourishes *'transcendence'* in this sense has to do with presence to myself, and so with memory… to affirm that one is 'spirit'… involves the owning, the recovering of a past, a liberating memory.[8]

Here, Williams seems to be arguing that the sort of thinking that allows us to connect with the past is transcendent because it takes us beyond the present moment. We obviously need memory for this sort of thinking, and this means there must be something deeply spiritual about memory.

Imagination and transcendence

Remembering the past helps us to see how the future could be different. When the prodigal son is feeding the pigs, he is able to imagine that things could be different, indeed better, because he *remembers* how life had been at home in his father's house. This enables him to transcend his dire situation, where he is utterly stuck in a pile of pig muck. Transcendence is all about moving beyond, so it's no accident that the young man says to himself, 'I will get up and go…' (Luke 15:17–18).

If we have forgotten our past, this sort of imagining will be nigh on impossible for us. Even if we do remember it, we may not be able to use our knowledge well. Recall from Chapter 2 that people with frontotemporal dementia lose 'executive functions'—the ability to plan and enact goals. This means that, although they may remember the past, they can't bring it to bear on thoughts about the future. So they too lose the capacity to transcend. For these individuals there is a particular difficulty with going beyond one point of view, whereas for people with Alzheimer's disease there is a particular difficulty with rising above the present moment. Both groups have a problem in placing themselves in a meaningful and benevolent story. It may help here to come back to the plight of the prodigal son. If his *story* is to end happily he must find his way safely home; for this he needs both to *remember* his home and to *work out and enact a plan* for getting there.

As Rowan Williams points out, if we can't transcend we become prisoners in all sorts of ways, ground down by the immediacy of our situation or enslaved to our own point of view, with no way of envisioning an alternative that might give us hope. Unable to help ourselves, we might say with the apostle Paul, 'Wretched man that I am! Who will rescue me from this body of death?' (Romans 7:24). In Chapter 3 we saw that this is precisely the view of dementia that is held by many—a deadly and hopeless condition that robs us of our personhood because it takes away our ability to recall the past or plan for the future.

Nevertheless, before succumbing to this sort of despair, we should perhaps take a more critical view of 'I think therefore I am' and ask ourselves whether there is more to us than the stories we tell, and whether we are more than our ability to remember and plan. We look at these questions in the next two chapters.

Further reading

Dan P. McAdams, *The Stories We Live By: Personal myths and the making of the self* (Guilford Press, 1997).

Daniel L. Schacter, *Searching for Memory: The brain, the mind, and the past* (Basic Books, 1996).

Notes

1 René Descartes (1596–1650) first stated, *'Je pense, donc je suis'*, as the culmination of an argument presented in his 1637 work, *Discourse on Method*. R. Descartes, *Discourse on Method and Related Writings* (Penguin Classics, 1999).

2 J.A. Singer and P. Salovey, *The Remembered Self: Emotion and memory in personality* (Free Press, 1994).

3 This is sometimes called declarative memory.

4 The technical term for this is semantic memory.

5 The technical term for this is episodic memory.

6 This is how Chris Roberts sums up his experience of early-onset dementia: www.bbc.co.uk/news/resources/idt-32ffb928-7d66-46bc-b73c-041c88b3807d (retrieved 10 June 2016).

7 J. Collicutt, 'Psychology, religion and spirituality' (opinion piece), *The Psychologist,* 24 (2011), pp. 250–51.

8 R. Williams, *Resurrection: Interpreting the Easter gospel* (Darton, Longman and Todd, 2014), pp. 31–32 (my italics).

Chapter 5

Beyond 'I think therefore I am'

Several things come together to make us who we are. Ironically, the one that is most easily overlooked is our physical embodiment and appearance, the structures of our material being. We may change greatly over the years, but it is often possible to trace some constant features: characteristic bone structure, the colour and expression of the eyes, the hands and feet. And of course our bodies are bounded. There is a point where I cease and empty space or another object or person begins. We are exquisitely sensitive to our bodily boundaries; every touch is a potential violation. The silence in a London tube-train carriage is regularly broken by a single word—'Sorry.' We say it automatically when we accidentally touch another human being, because at some level we are aware that we are intruding into a place that is them and not us, and where no one should venture without invitation or permission. *I have my body therefore I am*.

But our bodies do more than exist. They are the vehicles for our individualised way of doing things: our voice and accent, our facial expressions, our characteristic gait. When the father of the prodigal son saw him 'while he was still far off' (Luke 15:20), it was probably the young man's gait that he recognised. We each have our own personal style, temperamental dispositions, aptitudes and natural preferences— and the freedom to pursue these. We have values and aspirations.[1] *I have my devices and desires therefore I am*.

We also have a place in our social and geographical setting: *I belong therefore I am*. We live somewhere. We belong to tribes (for example, as supporters of a particular football team). We take on roles in public and domestic spheres. Sometimes these roles are formally recognised (for example, head teacher); often they are tacit (for example, the one people usually turn to for sensible advice). These roles can be so much a part of us that we feel profoundly less ourselves if we are not able to inhabit or exercise them. (Incidentally, this is a cause of much conflict in church communities.)

Sadly, as with our story, all these things are potentially affected, if not subjected to a full-frontal assault, by dementia. When I can no longer care for myself, others enter my personal space and cross the boundaries of my body to administer physical care. If the light has gone out of my eyes, if I shuffle about instead of striding confidently, if I have become irritable or querulous instead of gentle and outgoing, and if I don't knit or love to follow the tennis any more, my personality has changed. If I am housed in a secure residential setting, and if others have control of my affairs, my liberty is restricted. If I am no longer in my home, or my home town, and if I can no longer function as the secretary of the bowls club, as a grandparent or as the peacemaker in family disputes, I have relinquished my previous social and geographical place (and taken on a new one—demented resident of an institution in a distant town).

It is perhaps not surprising that Shakespeare describes the last stage of life as a place where all has been lost and mental life ceases altogether. It:

Is second childishness and mere oblivion,
Sans teeth, sans eyes, sans taste, sans everything.[2]

Yet Shakespeare was wrong about old age in general and dementia in particular. Even when so much of what makes me myself has been stripped away, I do not sink into oblivion. I continue to think. The thinking may not be rational and coherent; it is likely to be fragmentary and largely unconscious. But one thing is certain: it will involve my emotions. *I feel therefore I am*.

Thinking outside the airing cupboard: implicit memory

Chapter 4 explored explicit memory in some detail. This is the most obvious sort of memory, tested in memory clinics by asking people to recall a list of random words or a name and address; to draw a design they have copied earlier; or to select a picture they have seen before from others they have not. It is the stuff of our story. Yet explicit memory is only one of several types of memory. Figure 13 below gives an overview of the main types and how they relate to each other. This reminds us that there is one more type of memory left to be explored: implicit memory.

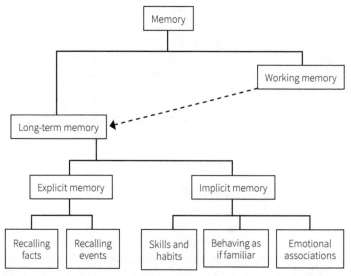

Figure 13 Flow chart of different sorts of memory.

Implicit memory refers to the sorts of memories that you don't know you know. For example, while at church I might open my hymn book and see a hymn whose title and first line I don't recognise, but when the organ starts up I am surprised to find myself joining in the words and the tune quite confidently.

There are several sorts of implicit memory, and the three most important are indicated in the figure. The first of these is memory for motor skills such as riding a bicycle.[3] People say that you never forget these sorts of skills. Last year I had to do some knitting. I hadn't knitted for a long time and, as I read the pattern instructions, I wondered if I could remember how to cast on. I looked down and saw that, without noticing, I had already cast on several stitches. It was as if my fingers had remembered what to do without my having to think about it—and in fact, once I started thinking about it, my fingers became less confident.

Another type of implicit memory is acting as if you were familiar with something without being aware that you had encountered it before. Singing an unrecognised hymn is one example, but there are many others: knowing the way around an area or a house that you don't recall having visited before, or finishing a crossword puzzle very quickly without realising that this is because you have done it before.

Finally, there is 'classical conditioning', first reported by Ivan Pavlov whose laboratory dogs learnt to salivate in response to a bell that signalled feeding time. This sort of learning involves our emotions and appetites. It's what makes us afraid of certain places or things that we associate with bad experiences (for example, learning to fear dogs after having been bitten by one). It's what makes us feel pleasure when we encounter a smell or taste that brings back the warmth and security of childhood—a sense of being safely at home evoked by the taste of Mum's signature comfort food. These emotional memories are deeply evocative; in our family, the smell of roasting gammon basted in cloves, ginger and honey instantly evokes feelings of Christmas Eve.

The producers of room fragrances shamelessly capitalise on this aspect of our psychology. Often we know why a certain taste, or smell, or sound makes us feel happy, wistful or afraid because we can recall its origin in an incident from our past. But even if we forget the original incident, our emotional reaction may well linger on.

Just as explicit memory is the basis of conscious reflective thinking, implicit memory, based on skills, familiarity and feelings, is the basis of intuitive thinking.[4] We use intuitive thinking a lot in our social relationships—deciding if we can trust somebody, or whether that person is just chatting to us or chatting us up, or what the right thing is to say or do in that tricky situation. Intuitive thinking is quick rather than deliberate and considered. It is based on hunches and gut feelings rather than arguments. It's really difficult to put into words. It relates to raw experience rather than theoretical facts. It feels more like 'heart knowledge' than 'head knowledge'. It's at the same time deeply compelling yet hard to explain to ourselves or others. These qualities are well summed up in an old nursery rhyme:

> I do not like thee, Doctor Fell,
> The reason why—I cannot tell;
> But this I know, and know full well,
> I do not like thee, Doctor Fell.[5]

Most of us have said things like, 'I can't put my finger on the reason, but that house gives me the creeps,' or 'Yes, I know he hasn't actually said or done anything to indicate it, but he's obviously in love with you.' When we do this we are using intuitive thinking, and this in turn relies on implicit memory.

The unravelling of the rich tapestry of memory

All the different types of memory and thinking are normally woven together seamlessly to make a rich tapestry of mental life, involving both intuition and reflection. But sometimes we experience them working separately from each other (as I did when I found myself knitting while wondering how to knit). It's a common experience to wake up in the morning with a strange feeling of dread, only to recall several seconds later that you have something horrible looming later that day, such as a dental appointment for root canal work. In this sort of experience your implicit memory has kicked in before your rather slower-acting explicit memory has enabled you to recall the reason for your bad feeling so that you can make sense of it.

We might think of implicit memory as a more 'primitive' memory system. We share this sort of memory with animals (recall Pavlov's dogs), and it's the sort of memory that is relied on in infancy before we can use words. Implicit memory is vital for our survival because through it we learn very quickly what will hurt us and what will give us pleasure and a sense of security. We learn whom to trust and whom to fear.

The different types of memory depend on different brain structures and pathways. Explicit memory depends on the hippocampus. In Chapter 2 we saw that this is important in putting memories for facts and events into storage and retrieving the stored memories. Implicit emotional learning depends on some other structures quite close to the hippocampus in the limbic system. The most important of these is the pair of amygdalae (amygdala is the singular, and the name means 'almond shaped'. See Figure 14). The amygdala is crucial in learning to be afraid. Put simply, if you wake up in the morning with a feeling of dread, it will be thanks to your amygdala; when you start to realise what that dread is all about, it will be thanks to your hippocampus.

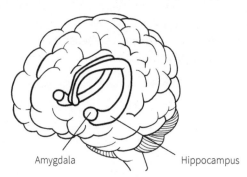

Amygdala   Hippocampus

Figure 14 Amygdala and hippocampus within the brain.

Following injury or illness it is possible for the hippocampus to become damaged but for the amygdala to remain intact. When this happens, the affected individual will experience the feelings associated with past incidents in her life, but will not have the capacity to make sense of these feelings because she will have forgotten the incidents themselves.

An early and (in)famous report of this phenomenon was published in 1911 by Swiss neurologist Edouard Claparède.[6] He had a female patient with very severe amnesia due to a brain condition.[7] She had met Claparède on several occasions but never recalled having met him before. On one of these occasions he shook her hand as if being introduced for the first time. Unknown to her, Claparède had concealed a pin in his hand; it pierced the woman's palm eliciting brief but sharp pain. Within minutes she had forgotten the encounter, and when he returned she greeted him as a new acquaintance. However, *she absolutely refused to shake his hand.* When he asked her the reason for this, she is reported to have said, 'Doesn't one have the right to withdraw her hand?... Sometimes pins are hidden in people's hands,'[8] but she also insisted that nobody had ever actually stuck a pin into her hand. It appears that Professor Claparède was her version of Dr Fell.

While this woman did not have Alzheimer's disease, the unravelling of the tapestry of her memory is very similar to that of people in the middle to advanced stages of Alzheimer's and related conditions such as Lewy body dementia. Alzheimer's disease damages some types of memory and spares others, and this is illustrated in Figure 15 below.

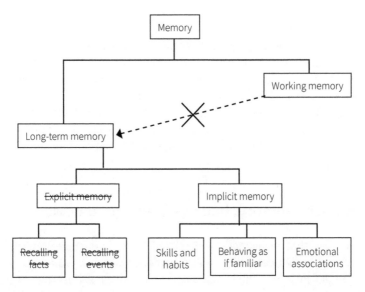

Figure 15 Flow chart showing broken connection between long-term and working memory.

We see that Alzheimer's disease targets explicit memory—memory for facts and events—and leaves implicit memory relatively untouched. It also leaves working memory relatively intact in itself, but the link with more permanent memory stores is broken—rote learning no longer works. This is why affected individuals repeat the same question again and again; the answer cannot pass from working memory into permanent storage. This makes sense; the brain-fade signature of Alzheimer's disease would lead us to predict exactly this pattern of memory loss.

Understanding the pattern of memory loss of people with Alzheimer's and related conditions gives us a helpful insight into the nature of their inner experience. As the condition advances, their memories will become largely emotional, and the few conscious reflective memories they do retain are likely to relate to things that happened a long time ago.

The shape and pattern of their stories will change. A person with dementia may no longer be able to construct a word-based continuous narrative, either for himself or to share with those around him, but there will still be a story. It will instead be expressed through basic habits, semi-preserved skills and gut feelings. The story won't be a coherent whole; it will be a series of flashbulb memories, of inchoate moods and fragments of purposeful behaviour. Caring well for a person with dementia requires the skill of entering into this kind of story and the willingness to receive it.

Implicit memory: bad news and good news

The way that Alzheimer's and related conditions spare implicit memory while decimating explicit memory is in some respects bad news. If I am in that situation, I will be able to retain bad feelings, but because I have lost the ability to reflect on them, I won't be able to rationalise and make sense of them, so I won't be able to put them in perspective. It's as if I am stuck with that feeling of dread, but unable to understand that it relates to a dental appointment that is necessary and will be completed in due course. People with Alzheimer's disease remember pain and rough handling, and they can come to associate these feelings with certain people and places. However, they can't fully explain themselves and tend simply to react with distress. They are not in a state of blissful forgetfulness but instead at the mercy of partial recollections, which can have the quality of nightmares.

While this is worrying, it does alert us to the fact that the way these individuals are treated matters not just in theory but in practical reality. They are not oblivious and insensible. When we insist that people with dementia should be treated with gentleness and dignity, even if they don't appear to recall what is happening to them, we are not just setting up some unrealistic aspiration based only on ideology (important though that is)—science is on our side. The way you treat people with even very advanced dementia makes a difference.

The other side to this coin is, of course, a wonderful source of hope: we can make a *positive* difference. If people with no explicit memory can remember bad feelings, they can also remember good ones. Just as they will recall a cruel pinprick, they will also recall a compassionate caress. Even if our loved one shows no recognition of us when we visit, and will not be able consciously to recall the fact that she was visited, her implicit memory will ensure she holds within her the sense of companionship, kindness and shared pleasure that the visit involved. Even if nothing is said, our presence—sharing a cup of tea, looking with her at a photograph, perhaps only holding her hand—will remain with her. The cognitive neuroscience of memory tells us *it is always worth spending time with people with dementia, even if there is no outward sign of responsiveness on their part*. They are made more fully present by the attentive presence of another.

Trapped in the present?

In the quotation on page 67, Rowan Williams describes the tragedy of explicit memory loss in terms of being 'trapped... in the present moment', unable to look forward or back. He sees this as a spiritual loss. This is the predicament of a person whose working memory is essentially intact, but who only experiences moments of lucidity, and whose story is held by the subtle mixture of feelings and habits that are the stuff of implicit memory. Yet perhaps there is another way of looking at this predicament. After all, haven't some of the great spiritual writers[9] talked of the present moment as a *gift*—one that eludes most of us because we are too intent on hurrying forwards to 'a receding future' or looking backwards with longing to 'an imagined past'?[10] Others have talked of the need for all of us fully to embrace 'life in God's now'[11] if we are to grow as Christians. Perhaps then there are some unexpected spiritual gains that come with dementia. A lot depends on your point of view.

Up until this point in our consideration of thinking and dementia, one point of view has been missing: God's point of view. As we turn and try to see things from God's perspective, new questions present themselves. Whose thinking is important? Whose memory is important? Who really holds the story? We can begin to entertain the possibility that the stories—the souls—of people with dementia are not only held by their implicit memories but also held, more fundamentally, in the memory of God. And when the flame of the human spirit burns low, and we can no longer recall and articulate coherent thoughts 'the Spirit helps us in our weakness... that very Spirit intercedes with sighs too deep for words' (Romans 8:26).

Further reading

Antonio Damasio, *Descartes' Error* (Vintage, 2006).

Notes

1 See R. Emmons, *The Psychology of Ultimate Concerns: Motivation and spirituality in personality* (Guilford Press, 2003) for a helpful and interesting discussion.
2 *As You Like It*, Act 2, Scene 7.
3 This is sometimes called procedural memory.
4 The technical term for this is implicational processing—see J. Teasdale and P. Barnard, *Affect, Cognition and Change: Re-modelling depressive thought* (Lawrence Erlbaum, 1993).
5 I. Opie and P. Opie (eds), *The Oxford Dictionary of Nursery Rhymes* (Oxford University Press, 1997), p. 169.
6 E. Claparède, 'La question de la "mémoire" affective', *Archives de Psychologie,* 10 (1911), pp. 367–69.
7 Probably Korsakoff's syndrome.
8 Translated by David Rapaport.
9 The most famous of these is Jean-Pierre de Caussade (1675–1751), a French Jesuit who wrote a book whose title translates as *The Sacrament of the Present Moment.*
10 Taken from R.S. Thomas, 'The Bright Field', *Laboratories of the Spirit* (Macmillan, 1975).
11 E.R. Obbard, *Life in God's Now: The sacrament of the present moment* (New City, 2012).

Chapter 6

God thinks therefore I am

How are we to make sense of the experience of dementia theologically?[1] For the Christian any approach needs to be grounded in the belief that God is our creator and redeemer. It also needs to connect with a Trinitarian understanding of God as Father, Son and Spirit. It needs to be compatible with the Bible and also to acknowledge the importance of the community of faith—the Church.

This may seem like a big ask, yet we already have some clues as to a promising way forward. Paul's words about the Spirit helping us when we reach the limit of our intellectual capacities (Romans 8:26) are one; his words about God's strength being 'made perfect in weakness' (2 Corinthians 12:9) are another. But the logical place to start is at the very beginning, with the creation of humanity.

God our mighty creator

'God created humankind in his image, in the image of God he created them; male and female he created them' (Genesis 1:27). We are made in the image of God. But what does this mean? Theologians have argued about this for centuries. Augustine of Hippo, whom we have already encountered in Chapter 4, wrote of a 'human trinity' that mirrors the Trinitarian nature of God.[2] For Augustine this human trinity consists of intellect, memory and love—the capacity to think, to remember and to be in relationship. This doesn't seem too unreasonable an idea until we are faced with individuals who do not have one or more of these capacities. Then it becomes problematic. Are these individuals not made in God's image? Or if they once had these capacities but have now lost them, has the image of God been removed from them?

One response to these questions is to turn to Jesus' command not to judge others (Matthew 7:1). He tells us we need to look to ourselves before pointing the finger at other people (Matthew 7:3; John 8:7). Also, and more fundamentally, he reminds us that only God knows and therefore only God can judge (Matthew 13:24–30; Luke 18:9–14). What was true at the time of Jesus is true now; even with our great knowledge of the mysteries of neuroscience, we can't read the mind of another person or look into his heart. Even if that person appears to all intents and purposes to have no intellect, memory, affection or even sentience, we cannot be absolutely sure. This is why people in vegetative states due to brain damage, deemed to lack sentience following scrupulous court inquiries, are nevertheless given both sedation and analgesia while their artificial life support is discontinued. As one surgeon puts it, 'In daily practice, physicians administer sedating narcotic analgesics to PVS [persistent vegetative state] patients simply because they are uncertain of and cannot measure their patients' discomfort… As science fails, we are left to rely on professionalism and the ethics of compassion.'[3]

So we can't be completely sure that any individual actually has lost all vestiges of intellect, memory and love in relation to his physical and social world. But even if we were able to be certain of this, there remains the question of whether that individual could still have these capacities in relation to God. The ability to think about, remember and love *God* (rather than the stuff of this world) is probably what Augustine had in mind when he talked of the human trinity; we are made in the image of God insofar as we have the capacity to relate to *God* in these three ways. In Chapter 4 we saw that this is what the Bible seems to mean by the human 'spirit'.

Is it possible, then, that a person may lose the capacities that underpin human spirituality as we usually understand it—becoming deficient in 'transcendence abilities'—and yet retain a capacity to receive the revelation of God? And might the reverse be possible—that a person could have a superb intellect, memory and capacity for relatedness yet still not be in touch with God? Swiss theologian Karl Barth (1886–1968) was convinced of it:

Is the revelation of God some kind of 'matter' to which man stands in some original relation because as man he [can]... take responsibility and make decisions in relation to various kinds of 'matter'? Surely all his rationality, responsibility and ability to make decisions might yet go hand in hand with complete impotency as regards *this* 'matter'!

Barth goes on to ask what implications this might have for people he (in the language of the time) describes as 'those, who as far as human reason can see, possess neither reason, responsibility nor ability to make decisions: new-born children and idiots. Are they not children of Adam? Has Christ not died for them?'[4] Barth is saying we simply don't get just how different the process of receiving divine revelation is from our normal human thinking, remembering and relating (Isaiah 55:8–9), and we shouldn't make assumptions about what is going on between God and a person who, humanly speaking, is incapable in all these areas. Barth's analysis is driven by a conviction that *all* are made in God's image, and that this does not depend on incidental aspects of their make-up such as their race or abilities. He was writing in the context of the rise of Nazism, with its philosophy of eugenics and genocide, and his horror at this deeply affected his thinking. Barth's approach is very helpful in many ways, though not without its limitations (the most obvious being that he doesn't specify exactly *how* people receive divine revelation). Perhaps his most significant contribution to the issue of dementia is that, by downplaying the role of human abilities, he draws our attention to a very important theological theme—the *grace* of God.

God our gracious sustainer

God didn't just make the world, wind it up and watch it go. From the beginning God has remained deeply involved in this world. God sustains the whole cosmos—including us—and without him it would cease to be (Colossians 1:16–17). Yet most of the time we act as if we have forgotten this, treating life as a game that requires a mixture of skill and luck. We feel as if we are essentially in control—that, when we encounter problems or obstacles, we can generally fix them ourselves or exert influence to get them fixed by others. When things go well we often feel this is due to our skill, or that we deserved a lucky break. When things go wrong we may blame ourselves, blame others or wonder if we are being punished. This is why, when we face an unanticipated crisis or uncontrollable adversity, we ask, 'What have I done to deserve this?' We are trying to work out the rules of play so that we can improve our skills, try harder and play the game better.

But, of course, this is totally wrong. Life is not a game to be played, but a gift to be received. It is God who is in control and who 'makes his sun rise on the evil and on the good, and sends rain on the righteous and on the unrighteous' (Matthew 5:45b). We don't get what we deserve but what God graciously gives us. It's not really about us at all; it's about God.

If we bring this truth to bear on the subject of dementia we can see that, theologically speaking, the issue is not the cognitive and relational capacities of human beings but the cognitive and relational capacities of God. The question then becomes not so much whether people with dementia can receive divine revelation (as Barth would insist they can) but whether God thinks about, remembers or loves them.

In Chapter 5 we noted that the capacities of the prodigal son to remember his father's house and to find a way back are important in making his story good. But much more important than either of these is the fact that the father has always had his son in mind and is waiting to welcome him home. The son's return doesn't take the father unawares; the father is watching and waiting. Even though, for a while, the son seems to have forgotten his father, the father has never forgotten his son.

This is one way we can understand what makes us human and therefore what constitutes the image of God in us. On this understanding, it's not about any capacity of ours at all, but about the fact that God holds us in mind. The very creation and continuing existence of human beings happens because God intentionally holds us in mind: *God* thinks therefore I am. This close relationship between God's active knowing of us, our creation and his continuing involvement in our lives is drawn out very beautifully in Psalm 139:

O Lord, you have searched me and known me.

You know when I sit down and when I rise up;
you discern my thoughts from far away.

You search out my path and my lying down,
and are acquainted with all my ways…

For it was you who formed my inward parts;
you knit me together in my mother's womb.

I praise you, for I am fearfully and wonderfully made.
Wonderful are your works;

that I know very well.
My frame was not hidden from you,

when I was being made in secret,
intricately woven in the depths of the earth.

Your eyes beheld my unformed substance.

In your book were written
all the days that were formed for me,
when none of them as yet existed.

How weighty to me are your thoughts, O God!
How vast is the sum of them!

I try to count them—they are more than the sand;
I come to the end—I am still with you.

PSALM 139:1–3, 13–18

In Psalm 8 the writer ponders even more deeply on the relationship between the thoughts of the Creator and their impact on human beings:

> When I look at your heavens, the work of your fingers,
> the moon and the stars that you have established;
>
> what are human beings that you are mindful of them,
> mortals that you care for them?
> PSALM 8:3–4

On the face of it, these lines seem to be posing the question of why God would bother with puny little creatures like us, but some scholars[5] have seen something more intriguing here: they suggest the psalmist is instead pondering what it means to be human—'what are human beings?'—and that he comes to the answer 'that *you are mindful of them*'. That is, we are human precisely because God is mindful of us! If God were to stop keeping us in mind, we would cease to be. It follows from this that, whatever our cognitive capacities or incapacities, if we are held in the mind of God then we are human persons.

The ironic thing about dementia is that, through its relentless stripping away of mental capacities, it reminds us all of something we might otherwise forget—our utter dependency on God. For those affected directly by dementia, this reminder may take the form of surprising experiences of spiritual growth, even in the midst of profound loss and suffering. For the rest of us, reflecting theologically on dementia offers us an opportunity to re-examine our assumptions about who is really in control of our lives.

The Hebrew word that is translated 'to be mindful of' in some English Bibles is *zākar*. It has a range of meanings that include 'remember', 'keep in mind', 'call to mind' and 'be concerned about'. It describes a kind of loving attentiveness, a calling to consciousness. It's what we mean when we say to someone who is going through a difficult time, 'I'll be thinking of you.'

Of course, this sort of thinking is essentially remembering, so it is not surprising that the Hebrew Bible has many instances of individuals calling out to God to *remember* them or their cause (for example, Psalms 10; 20; 74). In response, we have God's assurance that he will remember his covenant promise and will not forget his people:

> Can a woman forget her nursing child,
> or show no compassion for the child of her womb?
>
> Even these may forget,
> yet I will not forget you.
>
> See, I have inscribed you on the palms of my hands;
> your walls are continually before me.
> ISAIAH 49:15–16

The New Testament, with its radical understanding of the grace of God, goes even further. Our relationship with God is not based on our race or religion but simply on the fact that God knows us. This is strongly indicated by two almost throwaway lines in Paul's letters. In Galatians he tells his readers that their lives have changed since they have come to know God through their faith in Christ, but then he corrects himself:

> Formerly, when you did not know God, you were enslaved to beings that by nature are not gods. Now, however, that you have come to know God, *or rather to be known by God*, how can you turn back again to the weak and beggarly elemental spirits? How can you want to be enslaved to them again?
> GALATIANS 4:8–9 (my italics)

Paul is reminding himself and his readers that it's not about what you know, or even who you know, but about who knows you. Why did he think this? The reason seems to have been his own experience. Something happened to him on the road to Damascus that turned his world upside down. He thought he knew all about the criminal Jesus of Nazareth, but he came to understand that it was Christ Jesus who knew all about him. This was such a shock that it made him go blind for a while, but it seems he came to see this knowing as wonderfully affirming—something that enabled him to be fully himself, and which filled him with joy, delight and love:

> For now we see in a mirror, dimly, but then we will see face to face. Now I know only in part; then I will know fully, *even as I have been fully known.*'
>
> 1 CORINTHIANS 13:12 (my italics)

Paul was saved through God's knowledge of him. We might say that Paul discovered Jesus had always had him in mind. This is even clearer for the thief who hung next to Jesus on the cross and asked, 'Jesus, remember me when you come into your kingdom' (Luke 23:42). God's thinking not only brought these men into being; it redeemed them.

God our loving redeemer

Just as God's creation and sustenance of the world are acts of grace, so is his sacrificial redemption of humankind. We can't redeem ourselves by trying to appease God, or even by trying to love God. We don't generate love; we participate in it: 'In this is love, *not that we loved God but that he loved us* and sent his Son to be the atoning sacrifice for our sins' (1 John 4:10, my italics).

The language of cultic sacrifice in this verse from the first letter of John may feel a bit alien to us in the West in the 21st century, yet the day-to-day sacrifices made by those who care for loved ones with dementia are all too familiar. We see the regular setting aside of their own needs in order to pay full attention to the needs of their loved ones; hours spent in largely thankless acts of physical and psychological care, even drudgery; acceptance of the confines of the family home, or lengthy visits to often dismal residential care facilities, in order simply to be present and available. All of this can be seen as both self-sacrificial and redemptive.

This pattern of redemptive care is demonstrated by Christ, most clearly through his earthly servant-hearted ministry of healing and foot-washing. This itself reflects God's deeper sacrifice of entering the created order as a human being: 'though he was rich, yet for your sakes he became poor' (2 Corinthians 8:9); 'though he was in the form of God, [he] did not regard equality with God as something to be exploited, but emptied himself, taking the form of a slave, being born in human likeness. And being found in human form, he humbled himself and became obedient to the point of death—even death on a cross.' (Philippians 2:6–8)

As he underwent his passion and was finally nailed to the cross, Jesus experienced his own stripping away of capacities—an assault on his soul. His bodily boundaries were breached; he had been deprived of his liberty and was no longer the agent of his fate; he ceased to proclaim the good news of the kingdom and became silent; his ministry of healing (literally 'saving') came to an end; and he was taunted because now he was the one who needed to be saved. Above all there was his cry, 'My God, my God, why have you forsaken me?' (Matthew 27:46; Mark 15:34). In all these things, Jesus is in deep solidarity with those who have lost all, whose stories have gone wrong, who feel abandoned and who are subjected to a 'politics of revulsion':[6]

> He was despised and rejected by others;
> a man of suffering and acquainted with infirmity;
>
> and as one from whom others hide their faces
> he was despised, and we held him of no account.
>
> Surely he has borne our infirmities
> and carried our diseases;
>
> yet we accounted him stricken,
> struck down by God, and afflicted.
> ISAIAH 53:3–4

Into the land of forgetfulness

And there is more. Set between the death of Good Friday and the new life of Easter Sunday is a mysterious period that we know as Holy Saturday. This is a kind of twilight zone, a deeply ambiguous and shady space of watching and waiting. There is a tradition, dating from the early days of Christianity,[7] and expressed in the Apostles' Creed,[8] that Christ descended to what is probably best understood as the lowest place of the created universe, what we might call the underworld. This descent has been located in that time between Jesus' death and resurrection, probably on the basis of his own words: 'For just as Jonah was three days and three nights in the belly of the sea monster, so for three days and three nights the Son of Man will be in the heart of the earth' (Matthew 12:40). At its simplest this descent is a physical image for the movement between Christ's death and rising: Christ is like a skateboarder or ski-jumper who has to go down in order to develop the momentum for his massive surge upwards. However, there's clearly more to it than that.

The place to which Christ descended has traditionally been understood to be Sheol (or its nearest Greek equivalent, Hades). In the Hebrew Bible this is the state of being where individuals exist but are unable to understand, remember or praise God:

> Do you work wonders for the dead?
> Do the shades rise up to praise you?
>
> Is your steadfast love declared in the grave,
> or your faithfulness in Abaddon?
>
> Are your wonders known in the darkness,
> or your saving help in the land of forgetfulness?
> PSALM 88:10–12

Here we have a description of those who appear to be less than human, zombie-like, inert and unable to be in relationship with others—

essentially imprisoned in a shadowy twilight zone. Does it sound familiar? Yet, contrary to the psalmist's assumption that God's wonders cannot be known in gloom and obscurity, we have this promise:

> I will give you the treasures of darkness
> and riches hidden in secret places,
>
> so that you may know that it is I, the Lord,
> the God of Israel, who call you by your name.
> ISAIAH 45:3

And we also have this intriguing observation in the first letter of Peter: 'He was put to death in the flesh, but made alive in the spirit, in which also he went and made a proclamation to the spirits in prison' (1 Peter 3:18–19).

The tradition that Christ descended to the depths to be alongside those who have been forgotten by the world, have forgotten themselves and who are lost and imprisoned, and that he brought himself and his good news even to these folk in these places, offers grounds for hope and rejoicing for us all. It is based on a collection of straws in the wind that add up to make a persuasive case. The case is ultimately persuasive because it fits with what we know about the nature of God—the lengths to which he will go to seek and save the lost. The mind of God in relation to individuals inhabiting twilight zones is expressed in his pitching his tent among them:

> Where can I go from your spirit?
> Or where can I flee from your presence?
>
> If I ascend to heaven, you are there;
> if I make my bed in Sheol, you are there.
> PSALM 139:7–8

There is nowhere beyond the reach of God in Christ, and no state so low or ambiguous that it cannot be raised up by his transforming power.

We now have the makings of a Christian theology of dementia, based in an understanding of the triune God who is creator, sustainer and redeemer. How are we to live this out? The remainder of the book deals with this question.

Further reading

W.H. Vanstone, *The Stature of Waiting* (Darton, Longman & Todd, 1982).
John Swinton, *Dementia: Living in the Memories of God* (SCM Press, 2012).
Nancy Eiesland, *The Disabled God: Toward a Liberatory Theology of Disability* (Abingdon Press, 1994).

Notes

1 The ideas in this chapter are a developed version of material that appeared in an article in a special issue of *Crucible*, the Christian journal of social ethics, which was devoted to the topic of medical ethics. J. Collicutt, 'Some ethical issues in dementia care: Re-membering the person', *Crucible* (2012), pp. 7–17.

2 Augustine wrote about this idea in *De Trinitate* (*On the Trinity*) sometime after becoming bishop of Hippo in AD396.

3 J. Jones (reply to letter), 'Sedation for patient in persistent vegetative state', *Surgery,* 133 (2003), p. 122.

4 K. Barth, *Nein! Antwort an Emil Brunner* (1934) (English translation *No! A response to Emil Brunner's 'Nature and Grace'*, in *Natural Theology* (1946)), pp. 88–89.

5 B. Wannenwetsch, 'What is Man? That you are mindful of him? Biotechnological aspirations in the light of Psalm Eight', *Farmington Papers,* EI6 (2004).

6 See p. 44.

7 Acts 2:25–27; Ephesians 4:9.

8 He descended to the dead (literally, 'the lowest'—in Greek, *ta katōtata*).

Part 3

Thinking of you: the spiritual care of people with dementia

Armed with a multifaceted understanding of dementia, including, most importantly, a theological understanding, we are now in a position to think about the spiritual care of people affected by dementia. We need to ask ourselves how we, as God's people, can bring the mind of Christ to their situation.

The secular world is not without an understanding of the need to take spiritual care seriously. When healthcare and social care practitioners discuss the nature of spiritual care they tend to talk in terms of kindness, compassion or tender loving care.[1] This language, of course, has unacknowledged roots in the Hebrew Bible's concepts of *zākar* (being mindful of a person) and *ḥesed* (showing loving kindness). Sometimes secular practitioners even use explicitly Christian language (for example *agapē*[2]) to describe the tone of this care. Spiritual care is also often said to involve holistic or person-centred practice.[3] This involves attempting to see into the heart of the individual, and to respect him as more than a 'case', ensuring that all his human needs—their soul needs—and not merely his clinical needs are addressed.

While Western secular approaches to spiritual care owe much to all faith traditions, especially the Judeo-Christian tradition, they are not intentionally grounded in the values of the Christian gospel. What might a distinctively Christian approach to spiritual care look like? And would it be possible to express it in a form that would be applicable to and acceptable for the care of people of all faiths and none?

What follows is my attempt to meet this challenge. It is based on the premise that the good news of the gospel is the assurance that, fundamentally, all is well, or at least well on the way to being well. This was most famously stated by Julian of Norwich (1342–1416): 'And thus our good Lord answered to all the questions and doubts that I might make, saying full comfortably, "I may make all things well, and I can make all things well, and I shall make all things well; and thou shalt see thyself that all manner of things shall be well."'[4] Julian, speaking from a social situation of great adversity and privation, tuned into the deepest structure of the gospel, which is the message that, in Christ, God has reconciled all things to himself and has made peace with the created order (Colossians 1:15–20). There is cosmic *shālôm*, and with it the offer of personal existential *shālôm* for every human being. The bottom line is that we can be at peace.

We are also told by Jesus that those who are peacemakers 'will be called children of God' (Matthew 5:9). So **the core principle of gospel-based spiritual care is to be peacemakers for those for whom we care—** to communicate the message that, fundamentally, it's OK.

This core principle then needs to be unpacked in more detail, and to do this we need look no further than Jesus himself. How did Jesus communicate God's cosmic *shālôm*? He turned up. The message of the incarnation is 'It's OK—I'm here.' The reason we know about God's peace is that he came to be with us in life and in death. This is also reflected in our more immediate human experience. When we are trying to bring comfort, whether to a child waking from a nightmare or to a friend who feels lost or rejected, we are likely to combine the words 'It's OK' with 'I'm here.' So the first way we can be peacemakers is **to show solidarity through being present**.

The presence of Jesus didn't simply offer solidarity, vital though this is. He also embodied a challenge to the status quo. He was different and he made a difference. He demonstrated that things could be looked at differently and so actually be different. This opening up of situations by offering wiggle room and an alternative vision gives more degrees of freedom. It therefore brings hope. So the second way we can be peacemakers in situations that are troubling or painful is **to offer hope by making meaning**, or by making new meaning.

The third distinctive aspect of the way Jesus was present with people is that he made demands on them. Most frequently this is expressed through his command to 'Get up!'

> The Greek verbs used for 'get up' in the New Testament are *egeirō* (Matthew 17:7) and *anistēmi* (e.g. Luke 15:18). They can either mean a simple move from lying or sitting to standing, or they can mean rising from death to life. Getting up—arising—involves a move from passive to active, from relaxed to alert, from weak to strong, from sick to well, from dead to alive, from the world 'below' to the world 'above' (John 8:23), and—perhaps most of all—from lowly to exalted status.[5]

When Jesus instructs people to arise he is seeing their potential to stand tall, and thus dignifying them. Some individuals (such as the rich young ruler in Matthew 19:22) chose not to respond to this call, but those who did (such as Paul in Acts 9:8) became more fully human and more fully themselves. We make demands of those we most cherish because we want them to be all they can be (recall that 'Jesus, looking at him, loved' the rich young ruler—Mark 10:21); it is a mark of our care. It might seem odd to talk of making demands of people with dementia, but they still need to be stretched, stimulated and enabled at an appropriate level. This is a kind of 're-membering' of the person by the people who cherish him. Some dementia researchers talk of this in terms of the identity of the affected individual being 'extended' into the community,[6] for example by a community holding on to the story he has lost. We have seen that our being is created and sustained by the loving remembrance of God; we can, in a smaller way, also sustain the being of others by our loving 're-membering' of them. So the third way we can be peacemakers is **to affirm identity by intentionally re-membering the person**.

This threefold approach to spiritual care is grounded in the gospel of Jesus Christ and so can be fully owned by Christians, but it is stated in general human terms without using the language of religion. It therefore offers a framework for the spiritual care of people of all faiths and none. The approach is summed up in Figure 16 below. Here the three principles of solidarity, hope and identity are set around the core principle of peace, and each is summed up in a simple statement placed with it inside its circle. Next to each outer circle is a summary of what you need to do to enact this principle. The words in brackets refer to the way this can support the dimensions of human transcendence discussed on pages 65–68.

Each of the three chapters that follow looks at the practical outworkings of one of the three arms of the model, exploring different ways of being a peacemaker for people affected by dementia.

Figure 16 Threefold approach to spiritual care.

Notes

1   See, for instance, B. Goldberg, 'Connection: an exploration of spirituality in nursing care', *Journal of Advanced Nursing,* 27 (1998), pp. 836–42; A. Harrington, 'The "connection" health care providers make with dying patients', *Journal of Religion, Spirituality & Aging,* 18 (2006), pp. 169–85.

2 Harrington, 'The "connection"...', p. 181, uses the term *agapē*.
3 See, for instance, S. Hawks, 'Spiritual wellness, holistic health, and the practice of health education', *American Journal of Health Education,* 35 (2004), pp. 11–16; M.A. Goodall, 'The evaluation of spiritual care in a dementia care setting', *Dementia,* 8 (2009), pp. 167–83.
4 Julian of Norwich, *Revelations of Divine Love* (short text), translated by E. Spearing (Penguin Classics, 1998), p. 23.
5 J. Collicutt McGrath, *Jesus and the Gospel Women* (SPCK, 2009), p. xiii.
6 P. Kevern, 'The spirituality of people with late-stage dementia: a review of the research literature, a critical analysis and some implications for person-centred spirituality and dementia care', *Mental Health, Religion & Culture,* 18 (2015), p. 771.

Chapter 7

Being present to the person with dementia

Being present to another person means entering her reality. When the person has dementia this is quite a challenging task. People with advanced dementia effectively live 'in a world of their own'. These worlds are entirely logical, but the problem is that, as outsiders, we don't have the knowledge we need to understand the logic, so we have to feel our way in the dark for much of the time. We can sometimes gain helpful clues from talking to family and friends, but what we can't do is question the affected individual herself. We have to find other ways to connect.

Too deep for words

Words can get in the way when we try to communicate with a person with dementia, but this is also true of communication in general. There is a difference between what is being said and what is happening in an encounter between people. Certainly, in the context of psychotherapy, where the aim is to establish a relationship of trust between the therapist and the client, the deepest communication goes on without words, often in periods of silence and stillness. This is because implicit intuitive thinking rather than self-conscious explicit thinking is at work.

As we have seen, people with even quite advanced dementia retain the capacity for intuitive thinking. They continue to be sensitive to qualities of trustworthiness and benevolence in those they encounter. Person-centred psychotherapist Carl Rogers (1902–87) famously identified three attitudes that need to be communicated if a therapist's relationship with a client is to get off the ground: empathy (being willing to enter the client's reality); authenticity (honesty about oneself); and a warm, unconditional liking for the client. All of these attitudes signify 'it's OK': it's OK to be you; it's OK to be me; it's OK for us to be together. Where we are able to take on these attitudes, we will find we can connect more closely with others even when no words are spoken; we will be on the way to developing a quality of being fully present. Towards the end of his life, Rogers reflected on his many years' experience of therapy and came to the conclusion that presence to both self and to the other is the key to healing:

> When I am closest to my inner, intuitive self, when I am somehow in touch with the unknown in me… Then, simply my *presence* is releasing and helpful to the other… Our relationship transcends itself and becomes part of something larger. Profound growth and healing are also present.[1]

Rogers seems to be describing a situation when 'deep calls to deep' (Psalm 42:7)—a connection that is made simply by one being fully with the other in silence and stillness, drawing them both into what the Bible describes as 'the breadth and length and height and depth', and the knowledge of 'the love of Christ that surpasses knowledge' (Ephesians 3:18–19). It is a kind of wordless prayer.

Where people touch something deep together, intimacy emerges. We all yearn for intimacy, but it is a particular issue for those who are lonely (recall pages 51–52). Intimacy also seems to be a need that becomes more marked in later life, so much so that it has been identified as a distinctive component of the spiritual needs of older people.[2]

Establishing intimacy can be done quite quickly by attentive 'listening' to the body language of the other person and mirroring it with our own in a non-verbal 'being with'. This mirroring validates the being of the other person. In a well-known and very moving short film,[3] social worker Naomi Feil mirrors the repetitive tapping of a lady with advanced dementia in her own movements, and matches the pace of her singing to the pace of the tapping so that a sort of harmony emerges in the encounter and an undoubted connection is created between them.

Feil also uses a gentle form of touch, which appears to offer comfort and calmness to this lady. The touching of people with dementia needs to be approached with some caution. It is essential not to violate their bodily boundaries with unexpected or unwanted touch. Yet most older people who live alone and most people with dementia are hungry for physical contact that goes beyond what is required for personal and medical care. *It is important to ask permission before initiating social touch.* Where the individual concerned seems incapable of indicating consent, some warning can be given. Always approach from within the line of sight and say something like, 'I'm just going to hold your hand for a minute—I hope that's OK.' You then need to be alert to signs of discomfort from the individual, such as an attempt to withdraw her hand, or to push you away, or a tensing of her muscles. If this happens you should end the contact, saying something like, 'It seems you're not comfortable with me touching you. I'm sorry.'

It is best to limit touching to the hands, though on occasion a hand on the shoulder or a hug may be appropriate. *Hand massage is a wonderfully calming activity* in itself and is much appreciated by many people with dementia. The need for touch goes deeper than simple hedonic pleasure, though. It indicates a primal desire for skin-to-skin human contact, a desire that we have from our first hours of life. It is about attachment.

Listening attentively

The experience of people in the advanced stages of dementia can be summed up in the word 'lost'. They may feel as if they have lost their way and can't get home. They may feel as if they have lost something vital, such as their keys or their wallets. They may feel as if they have lost loved ones who may desperately need them. Conversely, they may feel as if loved ones have lost or abandoned them.

It is easy to connect with these feelings of being lost; just call to mind the last time you mislaid your keys, or noticed that you were no longer holding your handbag. Dread and panic ensue until you find the missing object. For people with dementia, this feeling is never resolved because they don't know what has been lost or where to find it. They expend much nervous energy on 'not knowing'.

When our children were small I had a recurring dream. My husband and I were in a restaurant having dinner and I thanked him for organising a babysitter. He replied that he thought I'd organised one. We both then realised that our children were home alone and immediately tried to return to them. But, as is so often the case in dreams, we never got there—the car wouldn't start, the road was blocked and so on. The dream was a nightmare, and it's exactly this sort of nightmare that can afflict people with dementia throughout their waking hours.

The reason people with dementia feel lost is that their explicit memory is fading. Sadly, this is the very thing that would normally help them make sense of bad feelings by taking their current situation into account: 'I'm feeling all at sea because my memory is going and I'm living in an unfamiliar care home.' Instead, they are thrown back on previous experiences, often from early life (from the bottom of the airing cupboard), to make sense of their feelings. They know they are in an unfamiliar institutional environment where people tell them what to do, so a reasonable conclusion is that they are in a school. They feel deeply alone in a way that they may not have experienced since childhood, so a reasonable conclusion is that their parents have left them there. My most distressing encounter with a person with dementia was with an elderly lady on a hospital ward who was crying because 'Mum and Dad have forgotten to pick me up from school'.

In Chapter 5 we saw that the implicit memory system is 'primitive' in the sense that we share it with other animals, and that we rely on it in infancy and early childhood before our explicit memory fully develops. As dementia advances, the affected individual comes to rely on this system more and more, and so becomes more directly in touch with emotions from childhood, the most important of which is separation anxiety. Children between the ages of about six months and three years old experience this emotion when apart from their primary carer (usually a parent).[4] They appear desolate at being parted, cry inconsolably and search for their loved ones relentlessly. As children develop explicit memory and conceptual thought, they learn that their loved one has not gone for ever but will return (for example to pick them up from nursery); they come to accept periods of separation and even to enjoy them. There is a certain phase of Alzheimer's in which these reassuring thoughts have been stripped away, and the affected individual is returned to the period of early childhood where separation anxiety dominates. People in this phase often voice repeated, touching laments such as, 'I want mummy,' and 'I want to go home.'

Sometimes the frame of reference that is brought to bear may be from a little later in life. It is not uncommon for people with dementia who are in residential care to believe they are in prison. This is an apt metaphor, but it may also be based on real memories. In his excellent short film *Ex Memoria*[5] Josh Appignanesi tells the story of an old lady, Eva,[6] who is a Polish survivor of the Warsaw ghetto and finds herself trapped in a care home from which she longs to escape. Significantly, the first words she utters are, 'It is time to go home now.' We see the rather well-appointed care home through her eyes as a place of incarceration, where people speak another language, touch intimate parts of her body against her will, wield threatening machinery and will not let her go home. For people who have been stateless and have had to go through the insecurity of immigration in the past, apparently harmless questions about their date and place of birth (given to assess their orientation and memory) can be interpreted as the interrogation of hostile border officials. I have personally witnessed the fear that such questions evoke in older people who were immigrants to the UK.

We act on the basis of the reality we have constructed. The child waiting at the school gates weeps and looks intently for her parents. In *Ex Memoria* it transpires that, as a beautiful young woman, Eva engineered her escape from the ghetto by offering herself to a German official in exchange for papers. In the final frames of the film, having tried fruitlessly to escape from her ward, she again offers her body to a young male in uniform, this time a carer. It is a moment of great pathos in which the vulnerability of both is laid bare. 'You can do whatever you want with me,' she says to the young man.

Sometimes the anxiety is not so much about separation from loved ones as about duties that must be performed. 'Who's picking up the kids?' is a common concern. In her book *A Guide to the Spiritual Dimension of Care for People with Alzheimer's Disease and Related Dementia*[7] New Zealander Eileen Shamy tells the story of Jack, a retired dairy farmer with Alzheimer's disease. When Jack was not well enough to milk his herd of cows himself, his elderly mother would do this for him. However, as she got older, she became unreliable and he needed to check she had remembered to do it. Now a resident in an urban care home, Jack initiates little in the way of speech or action. However, at 4.00 pm every day he becomes restless and appears frustrated, reaching out to anyone passing by and asking, 'Mum! Are the cows in?' Shamy describes the way his behaviour becomes more agitated and his cries become louder, causing unease and embarrassment to the other residents and staff (who incidentally do not know his backstory). Their response is to give him a wide berth at this time in the afternoon.

Yet Jack's behaviour is logical given the reality he inhabits; he has lost something, and the nearest thing from his past to this kind of anxiety at not knowing was his worry when his mother was due to bring the cows in for milking. He brings his existing frame of reference to bear on his current feelings and he acts on it. If Jack were not confined to his chair by his physical frailty, he would no doubt be trying to get out of the care home in order to go to the cowshed.

Shamy goes on to describe the response of a visiting pastor to Jack's situation. The pastor at first responds by respecting Rogers' principle of authenticity—he says honestly that he doesn't understand what Jack means. It is good to explain that you don't understand because this is both honest and humble; *always say, 'I don't understand,' rather than 'You are not making sense.'*

The pastor is then at a loss as to what to do, but acting on good intuition he continues the conversation:

Jack:	Mum! Are the cows in?
Pastor:	Yes! The cows are all in. Don't worry now. The cows are in.
Jack:	Oh, thank you.
Pastor:	It's important to get them in on time.
Jack:	Yes, thank you.
Pastor:	I'm glad the cows are in.
Jack:	Thank you.[8]

As this dialogue proceeds, the pastor places his hand gently on Jack's shoulder and Jack visibly relaxes.

Something very similar happens in the film *Ex Memoria*. When Eva offers herself to her carer he pauses, apparently overwhelmed by the situation. Then he takes a deep breath and, placing his hand on hers, says, 'Everything is in order.' Sitting up straighter in her chair she replies, 'Thank you.' She smiles and her expression becomes peaceful. In a true British manner, he continues by offering to make a cup of tea for them both.

In both these examples the listener has managed to **decode the emotional significance of the words by being attentive to non-verbal cues such as posture, facial expression and tone of voice**. Each has gone with his intuitive instinct to speak into the situation of personal distress by communicating that 'it's OK': 'the cows are in'; 'everything is in order'. Each has felt the need to touch the distressed person to communicate in ways too deep for words that 'It's OK: I am with you.'

Going with the flow

Two main principles need to be respected in being present to a person with dementia. These have been described as 'holding' and 'validation'.[9] Holding is the provision of a space that is felt safe enough for deeply distressing emotions to be expressed without the people involved being individually overwhelmed or destroyed by them, or the relationship between them broken. It is a key part of good parenting, through which the child learns that feelings do not have to be suppressed because they are dangerous.

Validation[10] is to affirm the experience of another person by accepting its reality, power and subjective truth. This stands in tension with an approach that tells them they are wrong and need to take on a consensus view of reality, something that has been found to cause distress in people with dementia.[11] Yet we may be concerned that, in attempting to affirm the reality of affected individuals, we are not treating them with dignity but instead colluding with what is essentially a lie. Surely truth is important, especially to the Christian?

Here we need to focus on the idea of *subjective* truth. While it does not seem to be true that there are cows for Jack to milk, his feeling of worry is true. While Eva is not incarcerated in a Nazi police station in 1940s Poland, her feeling of acute fear is true. While the lady I met in a local hospital left primary school over 70 years ago and both her parents were long dead, her feeling of abandonment is true. These individuals will not benefit from being told about the objective reality of their situation; they won't remember it and it will not make sense to them, but only alienate them further.

The need is to reduce, not increase, alienation, and this can be done by **tuning into the individual's feelings and affirming them by naming them**: 'I am sorry that you are feeling so worried/frightened/alone.' **It is also important to be honest if you are unable to answer a question, but to keep a sense of presence all the same**: 'I don't know when your mum and dad will be coming. Shall I stay with you a while?' This is an example of holding; when faced with people who ask the impossible of us, our instinct is to withdraw from them, but this will leave them even more alone. Staying with them may not fully address their yearning for lost loved ones, but it will make them feel more connected for a time. When we are sitting with someone who clearly feels abandoned, our instinct will be to hold a hand, and this is almost always a good instinct.

Sometimes, as with Jack, it is possible to give a direct answer to a question that can feel like a lie. But, if we look carefully at the dialogue between Jack and the pastor, we see that the pastor doesn't specify *which* cows are in or when they came in. He also switches very quickly to general statements about cows being in, and he also shares his own feelings of gladness. In the case of Eva, her carer is quite vague about details, but his demeanour tells her that she need no longer fear. He moves to make a cup of tea for them both so they can share in the sense of peace that has been achieved. Of course, this may be a temporary peace, but if this scenario arises again he will be better prepared for it, and ready to offer 'everything is in order' at an earlier point in the interaction, thus pre-empting trouble.

In general, it is good to affirm the reality of the person's feelings but to do this in ways that don't compromise the consensus reality too much. Below is a worked example based on an encounter I experienced recently while visiting a friend in hospital. The woman in the next bed drew back the curtain and became rather agitated, muttering something about a nameless friend who was in a vague type of trouble:

- Acknowledge the feeling(s): 'You are worried about your friend.'
- Communicate the fact that you are there for the person: 'Would you like to tell me about it?'
- Address their concerns using words and ideas that that will work for them: 'I think you have done all you can. She is lucky to have a good friend like you who cares for her. You need to look after yourself too. You've been poorly and that is why you are here in hospital' (a bit of gentle 'reality orientation' slipped in here!).
- Provide comfort or diversion: 'Shall I get you a cup of tea?'
- Share your own feelings: 'I am very glad that you are feeling better about it. It has been *lovely* to talk with you.'

If, as I did, you ask someone to tell you their story, you may find it is disjointed and incoherent or clearly disconnected from reality. Just listen attentively, reflect back feelings—'Oh dear', 'That's sad', 'What a surprise' and so on—and gently bring the person back to the present without drawing attention to the fact that it is a different reality. You can do this by suggesting a simple activity such as a walk, looking at pictures, praying for their concerns or listening to music. This then becomes your mutual reality.

Sideways on

In Chapter 4 we looked at the airing cupboard analogy and saw that even after the door closes it is possible to glimpse and even retrieve some contents through gaps in the side of the cupboard. This is a picture of how lucid moments happen, but it was also noted that they don't only 'just happen' but can be drawn out in different ways. Sometimes when direct questions don't elicit a memory, an indirect approach can. I experienced this many times when I was in clinical practice. Once I was chatting with a patient of mine who had very severe amnesia. I mentioned his family doctor. The patient denied ever having met the doctor in question but a few moments later said, 'I wish he'd get his hair cut' (the doctor had a rather long fringe so that it was difficult to see his eyes). After that he was able to say quite a lot about his relationship with the doctor. He immediately forgot the conversation, but for a few moments we seemed to have stumbled or fumbled sideways into the airing cupboard. *So in certain phases of dementia, when direct questions are no longer helpful, a general, undemanding chat about the topic may prove fruitful in unexpected ways.*

Of more interest is the capacity of non-verbal media such as music and scent to, as it were, enable access to the airing cupboard sideways. A lovely example of this is the case of Henry Dryer,[12] who had been resident in a nursing home for about ten years due to a form of dementia that was unspecified. He was essentially unresponsive, unable to recognise his daughter and unable to answer direct questions. When given the opportunity to listen to the jazz music that was current in his youth, however, he became alert and animated and was able to talk at some length about his taste in music:

> 'I'm crazy about music, and you played beautiful music, beautiful sounds.'
> 'Cab Calloway was my number-one band guy I liked.'
> 'I feel a band of love, dreams; it gives me the feeling of love, romance!'

Henry not only joined in with the music, singing and dancing, using his implicit memory; it seems that aspects of his explicit memory were also, for the moment, 'released' by the music. He was able to reflect on his experience. Commenting on Henry's animation, neurologist Oliver Sacks remarks that philosophers have described music as 'the quickening art'; that is, it has the capacity to bring people to life.

There are similar cases reported with regard to scent, though it should be noted that many people with Alzheimer's and related conditions lose their sense of smell quite early on. Eileen Shamy describes a gentleman called Jim, living with Alzheimer's disease, who had become so unresponsive that his family had almost given up visiting him in his care home. One day by chance Shamy took a bunch of lily of the valley flowers with her when she went to see him. She found to her surprise that on smelling them Jim was prompted to talk at length about his garden. He responded to flowers like this every time he smelt them, and this gave his family a way to reconnect with him during his last days.[13]

In this chapter we have seen that entering the reality of another person can involve connecting with his emotions, all his senses and the frame of reference he is using to make sense of his situation. Not everyone will respond every time to these approaches, but even those who appear inert can benefit from the simple, calm and holding presence of another human being who is prepared to be with them for a while in 'the land of forgetfulness'.

Dealing with our own feelings

'Remember me in your prayers,' he said
And I accepted the task with gladness.
But now I feel the burden of his dread
And no longer can contain his sadness.[14]

Being present to the other person, holding and validating the most primal feelings of distress, can take its toll on the carer. That's why it is tempting to withdraw physically and emotionally. There is only so much of this that any one person can do, and we need to be well supported by others and in a reasonably strong place ourselves. We also need to allow sufficient time for this ministry, and not be tempted to squeeze it into an already busy life without making space for it. Feelings of guilt, fear, helplessness, frustration or just plain weariness can drag us down. Not all encounters with people affected by dementia end as happily as the examples in this chapter; taking leave of someone who is still clearly lost and in distress can feel heartbreaking. But remember, 'there are things in this life which cannot be fixed by you, or anyone else. Dare to believe that simply being present with people in the valley of the shadow of death really does make a difference.'[15]

This acceptance of our human limitation and the unpredictability of life is a mark of wisdom. Its fruit is that it brings us back again to the grace of God and the need to receive life *now* as a gift. Using this wisdom to make meaning for people affected by dementia is the topic of the next chapter.

Further reading

Eileen Shamy, *A Guide to the Spiritual Dimension of Care for People with Alzheimer's Disease and Related Dementia: More than body, brain and breath* (Jessica Kingsley, 2003).
Oliver Sacks, *Musicophilia: Tales of music and the brain* (Picador, 2011).

Notes

1 C.R. Rogers, *A Way of Being* (Houghton Mifflin, 1980), p. 129.

2 E. MacKinlay, *The Spiritual Dimension of Ageing* (Jessica Kingsley, 2001).

3 'Gladys Wilson and Naomi Feil': www.youtube.com/watch?v=CrZXz10FcVM

4 J. Bowlby, *The Making and Breaking of Affectional Bonds* (Routledge Classics, 2005).

5 Missing in Action Films, 2006.

6 Played by Sarah Kestelman.

7 UK edition published posthumously as E. Shamy, *A Guide to the Spiritual Dimension of Care for People with Alzheimer's Disease and Related Dementia: More than body, brain and breath* (Jessica Kingsley, 2003).

8 Shamy, *A Guide...*, pp. 137–38.

9 T. Kitwood, *Dementia Reconsidered: The person comes first* (Open University Press, 1997).

10 In the 1980s Naomi Feil developed a full-blown therapeutic approach to dementia called validation therapy: N. Feil, *The Validation Breakthrough: Simple techniques for communicating with people with Alzheimer's and other dementias* (Health Professions Press, 2012). While many of its principles are extremely helpful there is *as yet* no systematic research evidence for its effectiveness as a total therapeutic package.

11 B. Woods, 'Reality orientation: a welcome return?', *Age and Ageing,* 31 (2002), 155–56.

12 'Old Man In Nursing Home Reacts To Hearing Music From His Era': www. youtube.com/watch?v=NKDXuCE7LeQ

13 Shamy, *A Guide...*, pp. 75–77.

14 From 'Prayer' by Brian Thorne (2013). In *Accompaniment to a Life* (The Norwich Centre), p. 14.

15 J. Collicutt McGrath, 'Laugh at yourself—and get out more', *Church Times* (10.7.15).

Chapter 8

Meaning-making in dementia

Finding any meaning in dementia is a massive challenge. The dominant attitude in secular society and many parts of the Church is that dementia is unremittingly bad news. The only good news about dementia would be that a cure had been found. Meanwhile many people, such as the late Terry Pratchett,[1] have insisted that once dementia has advanced to a certain point, life for at least some affected individuals may not be worth living and the best outcome is suicide or assisted dying.

It would be wrong to reject these passionately held views out of hand, especially when they are expressed by people living with dementia, and when they are set out in a nuanced way, as with the story of the American psychologist Sandy Bern.[2] But there is another perspective to be had, noted briefly already in Chapter 5 and expressed most forcibly in the writing of psychologist Tom Kitwood (1937–98), which is that our attitudes to dementia should be reconsidered:

> Contact with dementia… can—and indeed should—take us out of our customary patterns of over-busyness, hypercognitivism, and extreme talkativity [sic], into a way of being in which emotion and feeling are given a much larger place. People who have dementia, for whom the life of emotions is often intense, and [who are] without the ordinary forms of inhibition, may have something important to teach the rest of humankind.[3]

This view echoes Jesus' words in Mark 10:15 about the need to become like children if we are to enter the kingdom of God. (Recall that people with frontotemporal dementia show some features that are characteristic of childhood.) It is an important message that needs to be heard more by wider society, and it can also inform the spiritual care of people with more advanced dementia, as we shall see later in this chapter. It is, however, not always a timely message for the loved ones from whom they are slipping away.

No sense to be had?

Being present to those affected by dementia includes being present to loved ones and carers. All that was said in Chapter 7 about tuning into emotions, holding and validating applies to them too. But, unlike the person with advanced dementia, they (usually) have intact explicit memory and conceptual thought; they will have a story to tell and words with which to convey their emotions. The emotions may include anger, frustration and fear, all of which are expressions of something that has been described as 'the long goodbye'[4]—grief. There is a bereavement-like process at work for both the person with dementia and his loved ones.

The New Testament offers us a model for how to be present to those who are grieving, in the walk to Emmaus story of Luke's Gospel. The pair of disciples on the road to Emmaus were grief-stricken by the death of Jesus. Jesus first 'came near and went with them' (Luke 24:15). He was simply present. He then asked them to tell him their story (Luke 24:17). Even though he already knew what had happened, he allowed them to express what they felt in their own words. Their story was a mixture of facts that didn't make complete sense, alongside emotions of sadness, perplexity and disappointment. Even though Jesus had his own different perspective on events, he didn't rush these disciples; he let them lament.

This principle is vital when dealing not only with family members and carers, but also with affected individuals who are early enough in the process of dementia to be able to engage with it using conceptual thought. ***There needs to be an opportunity for the articulation of emotion and the telling of stories.*** This process may well be repeated several times over the months and years.

It may be possible to help make some sense of the story by offering factual information. For example, where a woman with Alzheimer's disease has remarried later in life, it will be very hurtful to her present husband if all her talk is of her first husband. Explaining a bit about how memory is affected in Alzheimer's disease can help here by showing that this is a cognitive deficit that is typical of her condition, not an indication of where her true affections lie. This is why memory clinics and dementia charities[5] emphasise the provision of good information.

But, even with the best information, unanswered questions will remain: 'Why has this happened to us?' 'Why does it happen to anyone?' 'Is she still in there?' 'Did she really mean it when she said she hated me?' 'How long do we have to endure this?' 'Am I just her "carer" now?' *It is imperative to 'be there' with individuals in the place where no sense is to be had without rushing to make meaning.* This can be extremely hard—just listening, receiving the feelings and holding back on providing answers even when you think you have them. But it must be done.

One thing that can make meaninglessness tolerable is to see absurdity in it, to use humour and playfulness. Playfulness seems to increase in old age and can also emerge in dementia, where it can be cherished and developed as a means of supporting spirituality in affected individuals.[6] We will look at some of the practicalities of this in Chapter 12. *Engaging in playful absurdity is not done to cheer people up but to show that inhabiting meaninglessness can evoke something other than despair.* A clergy colleague recently told me of an encounter she had with a lady in a residential care home: on being offered Holy Communion, the lady's response was, 'I can't have it, love: I haven't been cremated.' It was a moment of pure silliness and they both just relaxed into it without needing to understand fully or explain. Absurd moments like these provide light in dark places, expansiveness in tight places and an odd sense of interpersonal connection. It has been said that 'laughter is the shortest distance between two people'.[7]

Once Jesus has listened properly to the stories of the two disciples on the road to Emmaus, he moves towards making meaning for them. He does not yet provide an answer, but he offers a familiar framework 'beginning with Moses and all the prophets' (Luke 24:27). *There are several traditions of Christian spirituality that can be gently offered to help orientate people who feel they are in a place of no meaning. These are not answers, but frameworks within which lament can be voiced and questions placed.* One example is the poem 'Dark Night of the Soul' by John of the Cross (1542–91). For John, true spiritual fulfilment is union with Christ. His strange message is that this is only to be found in our painful and anxious searching in the dark for something we have lost and for which we long; that which constantly just eludes our memory:

> *In the happy night,*
> *In secret, when none saw me,*
> *Nor I beheld aught,*
> *Without light or guide, save that which burned in my heart.*
>
> *This light guided me*
> *More surely than the light of noonday*
> *To the place where he (well I knew who!) was awaiting me—*
> *A place where none appeared.*[8]

This is, on the face of it at least, meaningless, perhaps even laughable, nonsense. But somehow when expressed as poetry it seems to offer hope in a place where no sense is to be had. Poetry taps into intuitive thinking and implicit memory. It has the capacity to signify meaning where prose and propositions cannot. It speaks to us all, but has a special value for those whose conceptual thinking and explicit memory are slipping away. The fact that thousands of people, not all of whom would call themselves Christians, have been helped by the poetry of John of the Cross shows that others have been in a place of meaninglessness and lived to tell the tale. It is possible to get through it.

Journeying into the desert

In my work with people affected by dementia I have relied on something similar to John's 'Dark Night of the Soul', but which is more akin to humour and play: the desert box from Godly Play. Godly Play[9] is an approach to religious education and spiritual nurturing based on the Montesorri method. It was developed for children, but is increasingly used with adults, including older people and people living with dementia.[10]

A whole series of Godly Play stories based on the Old Testament are set in the desert. In fact, the stories begin, 'So many wonderful and important things happened in the desert, we need to know what it is like.' This is fully in line with the Judeo-Christian tradition of journeying into the wilderness to seek wisdom, but is also an idea that is accessible to all. The storyteller uses a large bag or tray full of sand (the desert box) and continues to talk about the nature of the desert: 'The desert is a dangerous place. It is always moving, so it is hard to know where you are… People do not go into the desert unless they have to.'

One of the desert stories, based on Genesis 11–13, tells of Abram and Sarai's journey from Ur to Hebron. This is part of the tradition of all the Abrahamic faiths and so has broad appeal. Abram and Sarai are represented by two wooden figures. The first part of the journey is along the banks of the River Euphrates (signified by a length of blue wool) towards the clear destination of Haran (signified by a block of wood). After they have reached Haran, Abram and Sarai set out again into the desert, but this time there are no landmarks to guide them. The recurring question is whether God has been left behind in the cities. However, as they journey on, they find that God comes close to them in the wilderness, first at Shechem, then at Bethel. They mark these sacred places with piles of small stones. Thus the featureless wasteland starts to be populated with signs of transcendence. Later in Genesis, Abraham and Sarah (renamed by God) have grown old. At the end of the story they die, but we see that we are still connected with them through their many offspring, who are 'as many as the stars in the sky and the grains of sand in the desert'.[11] On saying these final words the storyteller runs the grains of sand through their fingers.

This is a story that speaks into many situations of transition, in which the future is uncertain and uncharted, but it has particular power in the context of dementia. The multiple modalities involved—hearing words; touching stone, sand and wood; seeing the whole scene; encountering danger, uncertainty, death and joy—allow people to connect in different ways and at different levels. The story offers a range of images and ideas that invite meaning-making. One of these is the idea that God is already in the places where we fear to tread; another is that Sarai and Abram needed each other; a third is that the story is bigger than any little, individual life and we are part of a greater whole.

The story has a shape. Both Abraham and Sarah make good endings, and are gently and respectfully buried. Later life has traditionally been seen as the time for getting our story into shape,[12] weaving together a number of stories to make a meaningful whole. Yet the way we do this is not straightforward.

In an interesting reflection on narratives in later life, practical theologian Ruard Ganzewoort observes that storying is done in a number of ways.[13] We need others to make our story with us, yet in later life many of those who journeyed alongside us have gone, and we are left to do the work alone. Others may muscle in on our story—'No, Mum, it didn't happen like that.' If we are frail or our memory is fading, others may actually seize the initiative and tell our story for us in a 'does he take sugar?' move.

The assumption is often that the storying which goes on in later life is simply looking back on the past, with the final phase of life as a postscript to the real thing and essentially distinct from it. Ganzewoort instead insists that the final phase of earthly life is not its epilogue but its *finale*,[14] a full part of the story or, as in the case of Abraham and Sarah, the culmination of the journey, which may be unexpectedly fruitful.[15] This is true for both life post-retirement and life post-diagnosis of dementia. Life storying goes on until death and, because it is also done by others, it continues after death. *The final phase needs to be fully integrated into the whole of the person's journey on earth. This is the task of meaning-making for affected individuals, and it is the task of meaning-making for those who care for them.*

After my father had moved into his '*oubliette*', he discovered a like-minded gentleman with whom he became firm friends. They were both in their late eighties. His friend belonged to a whisky club and received samples of fine whiskies regularly by post. The two of them spent many a happy evening enjoying these together, recalling the last days of the British Empire and discussing the politics of today. This gentleman spoke at my father's funeral. He described how people in their residence expressed genteel surprise on regularly hearing mischievous laughter coming from his flat, and he noted that laughter and joy were apparently not thought fitting in a residence for older people, where hushed tones seemed to be the norm. He then proceeded to read out a long list of the whiskies they had sampled together. This was not an epilogue to my father's 'real' story; it was its finale.

But my father was lucky enough to be *compos mentis*. Is it possible to integrate the last phases of the life of a person with dementia into a whole-life narrative? Here *we have to move from simply lamenting and reflecting on dementia to committing ourselves to a particular way of seeing it.* In the words of Godly Play, we need to acknowledge that dementia is a dangerous place; that people don't go there unless they have to, but when they do wonderful and important things may happen; and that meaning can be made and life lived well. This is a radical change in perspective of the sort finally undergone by the two disciples at Emmaus, when their lament and reflection on the scriptures had ceased. Now Jesus breaks bread with them and their eyes are opened to see things differently. It is the beginning of a different sort of hope.

Look at it this way: 'it is good for us to be here'

For the Christian, the key to meaning-making in dementia is based on the theology set out in Chapter 6 of this book: God is with us in it, forever holding us in mind and fixing his loving gaze upon us. In particular, the truth that life is a gift needs to be properly received. As dementia progresses we are entering a place where the normal markers of time are breaking down; where past and future come together in surprising ways. We cannot plan and we cannot possess, but we are caught up in the moment. We should not think of the present moment as static; it is more like a threshold between what was and what is to come. C.S. Lewis puts this well when writing of joy: 'All Joy reminds. It is never a possession, always a desire for something longer ago or further away or still "about to be".'[16] It has been observed that this is also a feature of Lewis's account of grief.[17]

The problem is that instead of receiving the present moment, we have a tendency to try to turn it into something else. We either look forward to the future or back to the past, or increasingly we try to possess or fix the moment by using a phone app designed for this purpose. There is a nice example of this in Peter's reaction on the mount of transfiguration. He rightly says, 'it is good for us to be here', but then goes on to try to contain the dynamic experience in three static *dwellings* (Matthew 17:4)—a natural but inappropriate move in view of what follows. *There are times when we all need to learn to acknowledge that it is good to be here by 'paying attention to the present moment without wishing it were otherwise'*,[18] and this is especially true as dementia advances.

The practice of mindfulness is based on this simple principle. It has been found to be an effective component of the treatment of a range of physical and psychological conditions that are made worse by our tendency to worry, judge or push away thoughts and feelings that make us uncomfortable. It is fairly easy to learn the basics, and there is a good introduction to the practice in the further reading section at the end of this chapter.

There are now some promising research findings indicating that mindfulness may be helpful in dementia, both for people in the early stages and their carers, and those with more significant cognitive decline.[19] Mindfulness has its origins in Buddhism, but it is increasingly being recognised that it also has roots in the Judeo-Christian tradition,[20] well summed up in this quotation from Jean-Pierre de Caussade: 'Souls who can recognize God in the most trivial, the most grievous and the most mortifying things that happen to them in their lives, honour everything equally with delight and rejoicing, and welcome with open arms what others dread and avoid.'[21]

In the Christian tradition, the nearest thing to mindfulness meditation is the 'Jesus Prayer'. The words 'Lord Jesus Christ, Son of God, have mercy on me [a sinner]', which are based on Luke 18:13 and said in the power of the Spirit (1 Corinthians 12:3), are repeated while breathing is slowed and the body stilled. Sometimes a cross is held or prayer beads are used. This form of prayer is meditative and simple, and expresses the deep truth that we should not base our confidence in our own capacities, but instead rely on the grace of God. It is a promising way to help both the person with dementia and/or their carers to be in the present moment. It is possible to pray in the spirit of the Jesus Prayer but to use other words that work for the individual involved. The phrase '*Marana Tha!*' ('Our Lord come!') is popular, and the simplest of all is '*Abbā*' (Father).

> The repetitive, basic sounds that make up *Abbā* are the sounds of infant babblings, of those whose speech is ill-formed, of those whose capacity for sensible language has fled: the first and the last sounds. They are [also] the sounds of foreigners…
>
> There is thus something wonderfully subversive about praying, or even breathing the simple sounds of *Abbā*. There is solidarity with those who cannot speak; there is solidarity with the outsiders who are welcomed by Christ into his Kingdom; there is an opening of the heart to the language of God; there is a relaxing on to the breath of the Spirit as words fail us, as they surely will for us all at the end of earthly lives.[22]

Whether we use a simple form of secular mindfulness or a more specific practice of Christian meditative prayer will depend on the needs and values of the individuals concerned. In the next chapter we will look at the importance of gathering information about these needs and values. For now, we should remember that not all ways of being fully in the present moment are religious in form. We have already noted the power of music to release memories, but it also liberates us to be fully in the present. *Simply being with an animal or a small child can communicate the message 'it is good for us to be here' more effectively than any words*; neither animals nor infants have a developed conscious reflective sense of past or future, and both have great capacity for displays of unconditional affection. *Whatever approach we take, it will be important that we too are learning to be in the present, and we could do worse than say the Jesus Prayer quietly just prior to the beginning of each pastoral encounter.*

Actions speak louder than words: the importance of ritual

In this chapter we have moved beyond being present to individuals in the darkness and desolation of dementia—showing solidarity—and started to explore the possibility of offering hope by making meaning. This involves enabling people affected by dementia to look at it differently. We are not simply with them in the dark place; we are helping them to find some points of light there. By looking at dementia differently we have a better chance of integrating it into the whole life story of the individual rather than treating it as a tragic postscript.

It is relatively easy to talk about looking at dementia differently. It is much harder to break out of how we habitually see the world and actually achieve it. This is where ritual has a vital part to play. It is perhaps the most powerful way of carrying out and achieving transitions into new ways of seeing things. *Ritual has the capacity to manage our anxieties, enact shifts of perspective, embed new ideas, invest meaning, express joy and above all make peace.*

Perhaps the simplest form of ritual, used powerfully at the end of the film *Ex Memoria* (see Chapter 7), is making a cup of tea. The familiar pattern of this action fills a vacuum, needs no explanation and marks the threshold between places of intimacy and vulnerability and the more mundane activities of daily life. People with dementia, particularly frontotemporal dementia, sometimes engage in what seems like aimless pottering, or compulsive fiddling with items (sometimes known as utilisation behaviour). It is not that difficult to inject some shared meaning into their actions by framing them as the first stages of making a cup of tea, going to see how the dahlias are doing and so on, and then helping them to do just that. It is perhaps not too far-fetched to see this as moving beyond solidarity into a kind of blessing of the behaviour—a benediction that frames it in a particular way and pronounces that 'it is good for us to be here'.

More formal acts of blessing are also important. A prayer of blessing is essentially an assertion that God is in charge of and looks kindly upon the person or situation being blessed—that 'it's officially OK'. In dark times, blessing is therefore *transformative*: notice that it's when Jesus performs a ritual action with *blessing* at its centre (Luke 24:30) that the disciples at Emmaus are able to see things differently. In some Christian traditions, only ordained priests say formal blessings, but anyone can offer a prayer of thanksgiving, which does the job of making meaning just as well. *It is good to consider blessing both the old family home and the new home when an older person moves into sheltered accommodation or residential care.* This can be a simple prayer or a full-blown service. Blessing reminds us that God is here (as Abram and Sarai found when they journeyed into the desert), and marks both the place and this phase of the journey as sacred. Blessing also links them with what has gone before and what will come next. *Blessing the person and anointing their hands with oil,*[23] *with reference to Isaiah 49:6, reminds all present that God has not forgotten them.*

Ritual is also helpful at more mundane transition points. Sometimes it is difficult to say goodbye or extricate ourselves from an encounter because the other person is distressed, or simply has a desire for constant companionship. One way to do this is to *say, 'God bless you', or, 'I'll be thinking of you', in a tone that marks this as the end of this particular encounter. The leave-taking can be further eased by giving the other person a small token to hold and enjoy after you have departed.* This extends the memory of the encounter and should leave them feeling less desolate. Some might describe it as a 'sacramental' act. I usually leave cards with a photograph of some aspect of the natural world or reproductions of works of art. These may include a short prayer or Bible verse. They should be small enough to be held easily in the hand. If appropriate, I may offer the person a choice from up to four (more can be overwhelming).

On one occasion I left small squares of white fleece-like fabric. These have the advantage of being soft and comforting to the touch. They were given out at the end of a worship session in a care home with both residents and some family members present. The session was organised around the Godly Play story of the Good Shepherd, based on Psalm 23, Luke 15 and John 10. As in the desert story of Abram and Sarai, this is highly ritualised, making meaning through a set form of words and actions, the use of special symbolic objects and the invitation to participants to engage in an active response. The carefully worded indirect questions at the end of the story include, 'I wonder if you have ever had to go through a place of danger,' 'I wonder what got you through,' 'I wonder if you have ever been lost,' 'I wonder if you have ever been found,' and 'I wonder if the Good Shepherd has ever called your name.'[24]

Such sessions provide a hospitable, safe space where both lament and thanksgiving are possible, together with a framework of story and action within which to ask questions and make meaning. The fact they are considered worth doing at all with people with advanced dementia is an assertion that dementia can be looked at differently. They are in themselves an act of hope. Even if the session content is too complex to be received or is too easily forgotten, there is still a piece of fleece to keep, to hold, to stroke; a tangible reminder that 'I'll be thinking of you.'

Further reading

Keith G. Meador and Shaun Henson, 'Growing old in a therapeutic culture'. In Stanley Hauwerwas, Carole Bailey Stoneking, Keith G. Meador and David Cloutier (eds), *Growing Old in Christ* (Eerdmans, 2003), pp. 90–111.

Simon Barrington-Ward, *The Jesus Prayer* (BRF, 2007).

Mark Williams and Danny Penman, *Mindfulness: A practical guide to finding peace in a frantic world* (Piatkus, 2011).

To help children and young people make sense of dementia in an older relative or friend:

Jessica Shepherd, *Grandma* (Child's Play, 2014).

Matthew Snyman, *The Dementia Diaries* (Jessica Kingsley, 2016).

Notes

1 T. Pratchett, 'When the time comes I'll sit on my lawn, brandy in hand and Thomas Tallis on my iPod. And then I'll shake hands with Death', *Mail Online* (3 February 2010): www.dailymail.co.uk/debate/article-1247856/Terry-Pratchett-assisted-suicide-Ill-shake-hands-Death.html

2 R.M. Henig, 'The last day of her life', *The New York Times Magazine* (14 May 2015): www.nytimes.com/2015/05/17/magazine/the-last-day-of-her-life.html?_r=0

3 T. Kitwood, *Dementia Reconsidered: The person comes first* (Open University Press, 1997), p. 5.

4 P. Davis, *The Long Goodbye: Memories of my father* (Random House, 2004).

5 For example, AgeUK: www.ageuk.org.uk/health-wellbeing/conditions-illnesses/dementia/what-is-dementia/; Dementia UK: www.dementiauk.org/understanding-dementia/; and the Alzheimer's Association: www.alz.org

6 J. Killick, *Playfulness and Dementia: A practice guide* (Jessica Kingsley, 2012).

7 Attributed to Victor Borge.

8 Stanzas 3 and 4 from 'Dark Night of the Soul' by John of the Cross (1589).

9 J.W. Berryman, *Godly Play: An imaginative approach to religious education* (HarperSanFrancisco, 1991).

10 L.W. Howard, *Using Godly Play with Alzheimer's and Dementia Patients* (Church Publishing Incorporated, 2015).

11 J.W. Berryman, *The Complete Guide to Godly Play* volume 2 (Living the Good News, 2002), p. 63.

12 E.H. Erikson, *Identity and the Life Cycle* (W.W. Norton, 1968).

13 R.R. Ganzevoort, 'Minding the wisdom of ages: narrative approaches to pastoral care in the elderly', *Practical Theology,* 3 (2010), pp. 331–40.

14 Ganzevoort, 'Minding the wisdom of ages', pp. 336–37.

15 Romans 4:19; Hebrews 11:12.

16 C.S. Lewis, *Surprised by Joy: The shape of my early life* (Geoffrey Bles, 1955).

17 C.M. Parkes, *Bereavement: Studies of grief in adult life* (Penguin, 1972), pp. 75–76.

18 R. Bretherton, J. Collicutt and J. Brickman, *Being Mindful, Being Christian: An invitation to mindful discipleship* (Monarch, 2016), p. 18.

19 G. Robertson, 'Spirituality and ageing—the role of mindfulness in supporting people with dementia to live well', *Working with Older People* 19 (2015), pp. 123–33.

20 Collicutt, Bretherton and Brickman, *Being Mindful, Being Christian*; T. Stead, *Mindfulness and Christian Spirituality* (SPCK, 2016).

21 See Chapter 5, note 9.

22 J. Collicutt, *When You Pray: Daily Bible reflections for Lent and Easter on the Lord's Prayer* (BRF, 2012), p. 61.

23 This is also restricted to ordained priests in some Christian traditions.

24 J.W. Berryman, *The Complete Guide to Godly Play* volume 3 (Living the Good News, 2002), pp. 85–86.

Chapter 9

Re-membering the person with dementia

To affirm the identity of a person with dementia is to see him as God sees him—to remember his soul and accordingly treat him with dignity. Part of this is to support him in expressing himself fully so he becomes more fully alive. Recall from Chapter 7 that the effect of music on Henry Dryer was described as 'quickening' by Oliver Sacks. It literally raised him up 'from passive to active, from relaxed to alert... from dead to alive'.[1]

As we saw in Part 2, the advance of dementia means the affected individual will become less and less able to express her identity and will need to be supported in this by those around her. The attitudes and actions of her community will be crucial in determining whether her soul is stifled or enabled to flourish:

> In dementia many aspects of the psyche that had, for a long time, been individual and 'internal' are again made over to the interpersonal milieu. Memory may have faded, but something of the past is known; identity remains intact, because others hold it in place.[2]

'This is my body'

The idea of identity being held by the 'interpersonal milieu' should be familiar to the Christian. Archbishop Justin Welby memorably asserted, 'I know that I find who I am in Jesus Christ, not in genetics, and my identity in him never changes.'[3] To be 'in Jesus Christ' means to be part of his body—the community of faith. This is a body that is made up of many individual members, but whose corporate identity is made real as they gather around the Communion table to share bread and wine. When, at Emmaus, Jesus took bread, blessed it, broke it and gave it to his disciples, their eyes were opened and they remembered (Luke 24:31). They got up (arose) and hurried back to be with the rest of their community, which was gathering together so that it could be re-membered (Luke 24:33).

In the celebration of Holy Communion, Christian communities are reconstituted through the gathering of their members and the communal reappropriation of the memory of Christ. Much of this rests on the notion of 'body':

> The bread that we break, is it not a sharing in the body of Christ? Because there is one bread, we who are many are one body, for we all partake of the one bread... For I received from the Lord what I also handed on to you, that the Lord Jesus on the night when he was betrayed took a loaf of bread, and when he had given thanks, he broke it and said, 'This is my body that is for you. Do this in remembrance of me.'
> 1 CORINTHIANS 10:16B–17; 11:23–24

Christians, then, are already attuned to the fact that identity is not located inside a person, but is something interpersonal that is closely connected with belonging. We should already have an inkling that remembering is not so much something that goes on inside the head of an individual, but in and by the community of which that individual is a member. It's an act of grace whose bottom line is 'It's OK: you are cherished.'

If people are to be cherished through re-membering, all the things that make them who they are (discussed in Chapters 5 and 6) need to be borne in mind:

- I have my body therefore I am.
- I have my devices and desires therefore I am.
- I remember therefore I am.

- I feel therefore I am.
- I belong therefore I am.

In the following sections we will look at each of these in more detail (with the exception of 'belonging', which is the subject of Part 4, especially Chapter 11). We begin with having a body.

This is *my* body

The New Testament was written in the more collectivist society of the ancient Mediterranean world, yet it nevertheless acknowledges and respects the boundaries of individual bodies. The thrust of Jesus' ministry was to heal those who came to him, rather than imposing himself on those who did not want his help, and there are accounts of his seeking consent from those in need (Matthew 20:32; John 5:6). The only recorded healing that involves unexpected touch is that of the woman with the haemorrhages, in which Jesus is the one taken by surprise (Mark 5:27–30).

When the Spirit is given on the day of Pentecost, it falls on the whole gathered body, but individual tongues of flame also rest on each member, indicating that individual identity is also important (Acts 2:2–3).

The place to begin in re-membering identity is to respect the bodily boundaries of the person with dementia, always seeking consent to touch and, where touch is necessary, continuing to explain what is being done and why. *It is always good to signal what you are going to do in advance and, where prolonged touching or intimate contact is required, to give the person the chance for a break.* Where possible, it is better to assist and enable rather than carry out the activity for the person. Given enough time, people with dementia can be capable of quite a lot, but they can't be rushed, and they need continual, gentle prompting because they tend to lose the thread of what they are doing. Yet time is a luxury many professional carers do not have, so they do what is quickest, thus disabling the person receiving care. Spiritual care respects the autonomy and agency of the affected individual and puts conditions in place for these to be expressed to the full. This will involve allowing a realistic amount of time to carry out the basic activities of daily living.

Choice is an important aspect of autonomy and, where possible, a choice of what to wear should be offered. However, *making a choice between too many alternatives is very demanding of decision-making capacity*. Never ask, 'What would you like to wear?' Offer just two alternatives. We express ourselves through clothing, make-up and hairstyle, and efforts should be made to keep these in line with the affected individual's previous tastes (always allowing for the fact that tastes change and develop naturally through life). This goes for other aspects of lifestyle such as food preferences. I well recall an occasion towards the end of my mother's life when I tried to get her to drink lemon barley water; even though she was weak, she opened her eyes and said sharply, 'Never liked it then—why should I like it now?'

As we age there can be a disconnection between our self-image and the image we see staring back at us from the mirror. This has been explored in a piece by Rose Mula entitled 'Stranger in My House':

> She's very clever. She manages to keep out of sight for the most part; but whenever I pass a mirror, I catch a glimpse of her there; and when I look into a mirror directly to check on my appearance, suddenly she's hogging the whole thing, completely obliterating my gorgeous face and body. It's very disconcerting. I've tried screaming at her to leave—but she just screams back, grimacing horribly. She's really rather frightening.[4]

Mula's piece is light-hearted in tone but it deals with a very serious topic—the distress caused by seeing someone you take to be a stranger in the mirror. Subsequent attempts to make sense of the experience lead some people with dementia to believe there is a person who may wish them harm living in their home. For this reason, *it can sometimes be necessary to remove mirrors from the environment of a person with dementia so that their sense of identity is not unnecessarily violated.*

Just as an unfamiliar visual image may be disturbing, being called by an unfamiliar name is a potential assault on identity. People have names that are used exclusively by intimates (for example, the only person who ever called me 'Jo' was my mother), and they have varying preferences as to the use of first name, title and nickname. A surprising number of people have a preferred name that bears no relationship at all to their formal names. (For example, someone whose legal name is David Alan Jones but who has always been known as Wally.) *It is important to ascertain how the affected individual would like to be addressed*, either by asking directly or getting information from other sources. One way of doing this is explored in the next section.

This is me

We each have our devices and desires: personal style; temperamental dispositions; aptitudes and natural preferences; and values and aspirations. Where we are unable or not permitted to express these or act in accordance with them, we will feel alienated and miserable. In contrast, where we are enabled to express them, our souls will flourish and we will feel that 'This is me.'

As our capacity to assert ourselves declines due to physical frailty, illness or cognitive impairment, we come to depend more and more on others to ensure that we continue to live in accordance with these very personal characteristics. However, others—even those closest to us— can get us wrong, and not everybody has an intimate friend or family member who can act as an advocate. It's therefore sensible to make a record of the key things that make us who we are, so that in the event of our becoming incapacitated and being cared for by strangers, there is a reliable source of information on which others can draw. After all, you can't deliver person-centred care if you don't know anything about the person.

One good way of doing this is to prepare a 'This-is-my-life book'.[5] This is a loose-leaf book that can either be handwritten with photographs and small items stuck to the pages as in a scrapbook, or word-processed with scanned photographs. The advantage of the word-processed version is obviously that there is a backup if the original gets lost or damaged. The advantage of the hand-written version is that it may feel more immediate and personal. The preparation of these books can be highly enjoyable. It is an activity that lends itself well to being done as a group and with young and old together. Young people are often interested to learn about the lives of earlier generations, and they can usually help with the information-technology aspects of the process. I know of a gentleman with dementia who was resistant to producing a book until the activity was reframed as being important for his grandson's understanding of social history; then he was delighted to work with him on it.

The cover of the book can be decorated in a way that is attractive and highly personalised. *It is good to write in the first person even if some or all of the words are not actually written by the individual concerned. This is in the spirit of attending to her voice, and it reminds all concerned that this is her life.* The pages can be built up gradually and organised around a limited number of sections.

Who am I?
- I like to be called…
- Personal history
- Likes and dislikes
- Skills and talents
- Family and friends
- I could talk for England on…

Where am I now?
- The residence
- How long I have been here
- Key staff
- Other residents/friends

What has been happening?

FEBRUARY

18
MONDAY

Grandchildren came to
visit. I felt...

19
TUESDAY

Vicar came and brought
me Communion. I felt...

20
WEDNESDAY

I had to go to hospital
for an X-ray. I felt...

Things to look at
- Pictures
- Letters or cards
- Poems and prayers

Even this basic information allows someone to know a person better. As memory slips away it can also be used to reorientate the affected individual. For example, if a person with dementia keeps asking where he is, instead of ignoring him or getting irritated through repeatedly answering the question, it can be helpful to say something like, 'Let's look at your book together. See, you lived in Manchester until 2010; then you came to live close to Sarah in Abingdon in your own flat. Last year you moved into Grange Court.' Looking at a book means you are not looking at each other; it is collaborative, and the book has a feeling of solidity and authority.

Another way in which these books can be helpful is in providing preferred ways of managing 'problem' behaviours. There can be real difficulties in communication between different staff members in care homes, in hospitals or in the community. Having a section that includes an agreed, transparent approach to certain scenarios can go some way to addressing this, though it needs monitoring to keep it up to date.

If I am upset: tips on how to manage the situation (for example):
- I sometimes find the sitting room too noisy and it may help to take me to a quieter space.
- I sometimes worry about my children because I forget they are grown up and don't need picking up from school any more, and it may help to show me pictures of them now.
- I often get worried about whether the cows are in. I used to look after a large herd of cows. They are all safely in now, but I sometimes wonder about this. It will help me if people reassure me that they are safe.

This sort of book would not be complete without a section on spirituality, identifying the things that give the person a sense of deep peace and well-being, so she is able to dwell in the present moment and feel 'it is good that we are here'. For some people this may be something overtly religious such as a prayer, a Bible verse or an icon. For others it will be more sensual: listening to certain sorts of music; a hand or head massage; contact with natural elements such as fresh air, water, soil, stones or grass; seeing birds in the garden; or stroking a dog or cat. For others it may be more relational: laughter, play or keeping in touch with a person who is or has been central to their life. This keeping in touch can be direct, or it may involve reminiscence through reading old letters, looking at old photos or interacting with objects that are significant for that relationship.

You may find it helpful to explore this area for yourself, and to reflect on what might feed the spirituality of your nearest and dearest. Personally, I would want my carers to know that the choral music of J.S. Bach takes me to a place of deep peace and meaning. (It would not be enough for them to know 'she's a classical music fan'; I could envisage myself lashing out if I were forced to listen to Mozart.)

My spirituality
- It is important to me to receive Holy Communion regularly
- I am a Muslim and I need to pray at these times each day…
- I just like to be still and quiet

- I find this prayer helpful…
- I like to hear passages from the Bible
- This piece of music/icon brings me close to God…
- I don't have a religious faith—being in a garden is the nearest thing to heaven for me

This is my story

This-is-my-life books are one way of expressing people's stories and helping them to remember. They are very useful but have some limitations, the main ones being that they are rather two-dimensional and linear in form and that they are heavily reliant on words. An alternative approach is that of the memory box. These are becoming increasingly popular as ways of working on issues of identity with individuals of all ages and also with communities.

It is fairly easy to put a memory box together and it is, if anything, more enjoyable than constructing a book. Again, it is an ideal activity for mixed-age groups. The box should be large enough to accommodate several items but not too large to carry around. A large shoebox is about the right size. The box can be covered and decorated in a way that expresses something about the individual or people making it. The contents should be a variety of objects that signify important parts of the life of the individual or community. It is useful to include a short written explanation of the items.

My memory box is covered in blue paper, as blue is my favourite colour and I was strongly discouraged from having blue things as a little girl. It contains pebbles from the holiday resort I visited every year with my parents in the 1960s, along with a photo of us all in that place. There is a small poetry book from one teenage boyfriend and, hidden in its pages, a pressed flower from another. There is a romantic present given me by my husband, a small teddy bear beloved of my daughter and some Lego pieces that belonged to my son. There is my NHS identity badge, together with a history of the centre in which I worked for most of my career as a neuropsychologist. There is my Christmas cake recipe, a favourite humorous book, a choral music score and, perhaps most precious of all, my Greek New Testament containing a card sent by my Greek teacher on the occasion of my ordination.

My experience of sharing memory boxes in a group is that we quickly establish intimacy with each other. People who think they know each other well are surprised to find out new and significant things about their companions. There is much smiling and some tears. There is a sense that the contents of the boxes are sacred—some might say sacramental—and that they are to be treasured and respected; that to open and share is to make oneself vulnerable, but also to connect deeply with others. It has now become my practice to say prayers of blessing over memory boxes because they can feel like an extension of a person's soul.

One of the nice things about memory boxes is that, although they can elicit stories and even be a way of entering the airing cupboard of memory sideways on, you don't actually need any words or explicit memory to benefit from them. *It is possible simply to sit companionably with a person with advanced dementia and hold or look at some of the objects together in an attitude of silent remembering.* The box can give focus to an encounter that might otherwise be awkward, yet it does not make demands of those involved. The fact that you have to lift a lid to get in evokes a sense of wonder and curiosity that is common to people of all ages.

Memory boxes can also be a precious legacy for those left behind, especially grandchildren who never knew the affected individual in his or her pre-dementia days. The box can give them a sense of what Grandma or Grandpa was really like. I know one woman in her fifties who insisted on including a pair of black silk stockings in her memory box. This was so that any future grandchildren who knew her only as frail and forgetful would understand that she had in earlier days been a vibrant, sexy and sensual woman, and that this was also part of her story.

It is possible to use the material from This-is-my-life books and memory boxes in a more systematic way, as part of a process of 'restorying lives'.[6] This is sometimes described as reminiscence, but it is more than a pleasant walk down memory lane, valuable though that is in its own right. It is an active review of life so far, reflecting on what has given it meaning and purpose, and weaving this into a continuing story. Australian nurse and pastoral theologian Elizabeth MacKinlay has designed and evaluated formal courses in spiritual reminiscence. These consist of as many as 24 weekly group sessions delivered as part of the activities programme for people in the middle stages of dementia living in care facilities. She reports that the degree of engagement and appreciation of participants has been high. This appears to be because 'older people in aged care preferred activities that included reinforcing a sense of identity and sense of belonging'.[7] The key ingredient may be participation in a stable group in which your story is both heard and held for you by others. As if to illustrate this, in one session a participant aged 97 said, 'I'm hopeless,' and another group member responded, 'We are full of hope for you.'[8]

I am entitled to my feelings

People with dementia are capable of profound joy—something we will explore in Chapter 11. For a whole variety of reasons, many of which we have considered already in this book, they are rather more prone to becoming distressed. When faced with this, our natural instinct is to try to help them become more content. However, this may not always be because we want them to obtain the deep sense of *shālôm* that is at the centre of Christian spiritual care, but because their distress makes us uncomfortable and we feel the need to put a lid on it as quickly as possible. This may be necessary to manage a crisis situation, or to avoid upsetting other vulnerable people in the vicinity. But people are entitled to their feelings. We would do well to reflect on some words from the prophet Jeremiah: 'They have treated the wound of my people carelessly, saying, "Peace, peace," when there is no peace.' (Jeremiah 6:14)

Our lives are full of emotions. They enrich our existence and are part of what it means to be a human being. After all, we talk about people who don't appear to have much in the way of feelings as being like robots. But not all our feelings are pleasant. Every day we go through a range of joys, sorrows, worries, irritations, frustrations and fears. People with dementia are no different, though like children they may experience and express emotion with a high degree of intensity.[9]

This intensity of feeling may be hard for others to tolerate. Yet the feelings are valid and should be acknowledged rather than negated. The lady in the reminiscence group who said, 'I'm hopeless,' felt hopeless, and it would have been no use—indeed, a kind of abuse— to have told her she didn't or shouldn't feel this way. On the other hand, wallowing in hopelessness with a person who does not have the cognitive ability to see beyond it is also a less-than-helpful approach. This is why the response of another person with dementia—'We are full of hope for you'—was so very apt. It expressed his own feelings in a compassionate act of reaching towards her. This statement amounts to, 'We hear your feeling (so we cherish you), and we offer ourselves to hold you in it and help you through it to a place of peace (to transcend it).' It expresses a kind of grace.

It is important to recognise the fact that people with dementia may experience distress related to their condition or for other reasons, such as mistreatment, loneliness or bereavement. *If we try to dampen down the distress without thinking about it, we may miss something significant that they are trying to communicate.* Discontented dementia[10] is not always a bad thing.

One fairly common scenario in which discontent is appropriate is the loss of a loved one, perhaps most commonly a spouse. The person with dementia is entitled to be told this has happened, and is entitled to grieve and go through rites of mourning (in accordance with her abilities). Of course, grieving may be complicated: she will perhaps need to be told of the loss on several occasions and may react as if hearing it for the first time. There may be some risks about her attending the funeral, which will need to be assessed and handled carefully. She may ask repeatedly where her loved one is. She may become depressed or agitated. This will make the whole process far more challenging and potentially distressing for family members. Nevertheless, if she is to be re-membered as a person in their own right, rather than simply as someone who is the recipient of care, their need to know, to inhabit the role of widow or widower rather than spouse, and to undergo the pain of loss, should be honoured.

My experience of being alongside people in this situation is that This-is-my-life books can work well. A page about the death and funeral of a loved one, written sensitively, containing an order of service, condolence cards and photos of flowers, can provide comfort and a reminder, avoiding the need to state the fact brutally. Alternatively, a scrapbook devoted to the life of the loved one that ends with his funeral may be constructed (the affected individual can be part of this if he is capable), and this can itself prove healing for those who are making it. People with dementia may retain a feeling that the loved one has died even if they forget the fact,[11] so a gentle reminder does not always come as a bolt from the blue. It may be possible to work through feelings in ways based in the creative arts[12] that do not involve talking or reliance on explicit memory. Each individual will require a tailored response in which the family agrees to work together and be consistent (not always easy in the fraught aftermath of a family death). *The key is to allow the affected person to grieve in his own way, even if it is painful for those around him, but to manage the process so that the grief does not overwhelm him.* There is surprisingly little work on this topic, but a really helpful information sheet is produced by Alzheimer Scotland.[13]

'Do this in remembrance…'

All funerals are a kind of re-membering of the deceased by the community, but this is particularly true for people with dementia, where hopefully the re-membering process may have preceded their physical death. Ruard Ganzewoort describes the Moravian Church's practice of encouraging older people to write an earthly life narrative that is then completed by the community at their death and read at their funeral.[14] Many people, whether Christian or not, believe the person survives death in some form, so even then the story is not yet complete. In Chapter 12 we will look at crafting funerals for people with dementia in more detail, but the underlying task is to communicate the hope that the story continues: that the unravelling of the personality that began with the onset of dementia will be replaced by a glorious, transformative reweaving or re-membering of the individual into all he or she is meant to be.

The calling of churches is to live as transformative communities in the light of this eternal reality by beginning to pick up the stitches that have been dropped, by acts of solidarity, meaning-making and re-membering—small or large. In doing this they are cooperating with the work of God's Spirit through which 'all of us, with unveiled faces, seeing the glory of the Lord as though reflected in a mirror, are being transformed into the same image from one degree of glory to another' (2 Corinthians 3:18).

Further reading

Elizabeth MacKinlay and Corinne Trevitt, *Finding Meaning in the Experience of Dementia: The place of spiritual reminiscence work* (Jessica Kingsley, 2012).

Faith Gibson, *Reminiscence and Life Story Work: A practice guide* (Jessica Kinglsey, 2011).

James Woodward (ed.), *Between Remembering and Forgetting: The spiritual dimensions of dementia* (Mowbray, 2010).

Joanna Collicutt, *Living Well in the End Times: A Christian resource to support people in making peace with the prospect of death* (Diocese of Oxford, 2016): www.oxford.anglican.org/wp-content/uploads/2013/01/OD705-Living-well-book.pdf

Notes

1 J. Collicutt, *Jesus and the Gospel Women* (SPCK, 2009), p. 95
2 T. Kitwood, *Dementia Reconsidered: The person comes first* (Open University Press, 1997), p. 69.
3 Personal statement issued on 8 April 2016: www.archbishopofcanterbury.org/articles.php/5704/a-personal-statement-from-the-archbishop-of-canterbury
4 R.M. Mula, 'Stranger in My House', *The Andover Townsman* (8 May 1997).
5 The Life Story Network offers useful advice on this and other related aspects of dementia care: www.lifestorynetwork.org.uk
6 G. Kenyon, P. Clark and B. de Vries (eds), *Narrative Gerontology: Theory, research, and practice* (Springer, 2001).
7 E. MacKinlay and C. Trevitt, 'Living in aged care: using spiritual reminiscence to enhance meaning in life for those with dementia', *International Journal of Mental Health Nursing,* 19 (2010), p. 400.
8 MacKinlay and Trevitt, 'Living in aged care', p. 399.
9 It is recognised that some people in some phases of dementia can also appear emotionally deadened and unresponsive.
10 There is a very good approach called 'contented dementia' that has done a lot to improve the well-being of people with dementia: O. James, *Contented Dementia* (Vermilion, 2009); www.contenteddementiatrust.org.uk. It focuses on a way of communicating with the person with dementia that validates their perspective in much the same way as is outlined in Chapter 7. In this way, stress levels in both the person with dementia and their carers can be dramatically reduced. However, it seems to be predicated on the idea that discontented dementia is a bad thing.
11 H. Gruetzner, J.W. Ellor and N. Back, 'Identifiable grief responses in persons with Alzheimer's disease', *Journal of Social Work in End-of-Life & Palliative Care,* 8 (2012), pp. 151–64.
12 B.E. Thompson and R.A. Neimeyer (eds), *Grief and the Expressive Arts: Practices for creating meaning* (Routledge, 2014).
13 www.alzscot.org/assets/0000/0176/loss_bereavement.pdf
14 R.R. Ganzevoort, 'Minding the wisdom of ages: narrative approaches to pastoral care in the elderly', *Practical Theology,* 3 (2010), pp. 334–35.

Part 4

Thinking about us: dementia-friendly churches

Chapter 3 introduced the idea of a dementia-friendly community. Churches are above all communities, whether gathered in centres of worship, connected through networks or dispersed as yeast and salt in the wider communities of the world. The pattern of the Eucharist mirrors this dynamic sense of community, in which people gather, network and are sent out 'in the power of [God's] Spirit to live and work to [his] praise and glory'.[1]

Communities are marked by relationships involving interdependence and mutual obligation. This means membership of a community has both benefits and costs. The benefits are the sense of connection, relatedness and access to common resources. The costs are the vulnerability entailed in letting ourselves be dependent, at least to some extent, on the goodwill and competence of others; the relinquishment of personal control to the common will; and obligations to other members of the community. Some of these costs may seem too great for people who feel they can no longer meet community obligations, or who find they are needing to increase their dependence on other community members. This is why people who become frail or develop depression or dementia tend to withdraw from community life, become disconnected and be seen as undergoing a kind of isolated 'private tragedy'.[2]

In this final part of the book we explore the question of how Christian communities can work against this narrative of private tragedy and become more dementia-friendly, both to people who would count themselves as already part of a church and to those who would not. Becoming a more dementia-friendly community is not just about making practical changes (though this may be a good place to start).

It's about the development of a culture that shows itself in the attitudes of its members. This is a sort of virtuous circle, where all the parts are important and feed into each other, as shown in Figure 17 below.

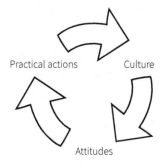

Practical actions   Culture

Attitudes

Figure 17 Virtuous circle of a dementia-friendly community.

Churches have much to learn from the secular push towards dementia-friendly communities, but they also have their own perspective to offer. They are more than benevolent voluntary groups or civic institutions (though they are certainly the former, and the Church of England has a special claim to the latter); churches are the body of Christ. Crucially, *the aspiration of churches to be dementia-friendly communities comes from an attitude to all people that is grounded in the love of God and informed by Christian theology*. This is why this book explored the theological themes of God our creator, sustainer and redeemer in Chapter 6 and used them as the basis for the approach to spiritual care set out in Part 3. We have looked at this from the perspective of dementia, but the theological ideas and principles of spiritual practice are applicable to people in all sorts of situations of difficulty or marginalisation. This is a really important point: *a dementia-friendly community is likely to be a community that is friendly to all*. This means that making a church more dementia friendly is not going to be at the cost of putting off other groups. It is in fact a way of making that church more hospitable across the board, because either the changes made will be applicable to all, or the thinking done in order to decide on those changes will be the right sort of thinking with which to approach other challenges. For example, thinking about how to make a church more accessible to people who no longer understand written or spoken language because of dementia will help in thinking about how to meet the needs of immigrants or visitors who do not speak English, or people with dyslexia or those with other learning difficulties.

We have seen that a dementia-friendly community is understood to be one that listens to people affected by dementia; challenges stigma and promotes awareness of dementia; and supports the engagement of and recognises the contribution made by people with dementia.[3] We might describe a dementia-friendly church as one that has an attitude to people affected by dementia that is grounded in the love of God and informed by Christian theology, and which has consequently made particular efforts to ensure they are and continue to:

- be fully included
- really belong
- be celebrated
- be connected
- be safe but not overprotected

In the following chapters we will look at each of these dimensions in turn.

Notes

1 *Common Worship* (Church House Publishing, 2000), p. 182.
2 S.H. McFadden and J.T. McFadden, *Aging Together: Dementia, friendship and flourishing communities* (Johns Hopkins University Press, 2011), p. 128.
3 See p. 50.

Chapter 10

Full inclusion

Gathered church communities should be physically, socially and spiritually hospitable to people affected by dementia. There is also a sense in which there needs to be a hospitable attitude to dementia itself. This may seem odd, but it is in the spirit of 'it is good for us to be here' which is part of Christian meaning-making and central to being a 'community of blessing'.[1]

Hospitality is likewise a characteristic of mindfulness. Mindfulness goes against the grain because it promotes an attitude of compassionate hospitality to that which we most fear and want to push away. Practitioners of mindfulness are encouraged to 'turn toward and approach painful experiences with kindness'.[2] The natural instinct with dementia is to do the opposite: to avoid mentioning it, to try to cover it up, to joke about it ('I'm going gaga') and to invest emotionally in finding a cure. None of these ways of coping with dementia is wrong; they help people get by. But there is also a need to come to some sort of terms with dementia, to befriend it. This may mean talking about it and naming the issue; however, there are also ways of making peace with the presence of the condition that don't require words but simply a culture of hospitable understanding.

Sometimes it feels difficult to help or even to identify a person with dementia because, at least in the early phase, he won't admit to the condition, or his family collude with him by compensating for his cognitive problems. This is an attempt to safeguard the dignity of the person concerned, and should always be respected. However, *if the environment in general is hospitable to people with dementia then an affected individual shouldn't require too much in the way of special treatment that draws attention to his or her condition*. The way to begin with this is simply to talk about dementia more.

Re-membering through remembering

It is good to remember regularly all those affected by dementia, together with the services that support them, in public prayers. The way we talk about people with dementia says a lot about our attitude and our knowledge. *It is generally unhelpful to talk about 'dementia victims' or 'dementia sufferers'; it is more appropriate to say 'people living with dementia'.* It is also not accurate to refer to dementia as a mental health condition or mental illness. People with dementia do not need the additional (unjustified) stigma associated with mental health conditions.

Simply remembering people with dementia can be a massive step forward, but including some of the theological themes explored in Chapter 6 is also helpful and comforting. For example, here is a prayer written for Dementia Awareness Week 2016 by Doug Chaplin:

> *God of hope and resurrection,*
> *you know us better than we know ourselves,*
> *and draw us to peace and wholeness in your love.*
> *We remember before you*
> *those who are unable to remember their own lives.*
> *Guard and treasure their lost memories for them,*
> *and hold their past in your safe hands,*
> *that when the death of the body comes,*
> *you may bring them to the full life of the resurrection,*
> *restore and heal the memories of their lives,*
> *and give them back to themselves,*
> *that we with them may rejoice in your love,*
> *and find the fullness of life in your presence,*
> *Father, Son and Holy Spirit. Amen.*[3]

It is, of course, also possible to express these ideas in the form of a sermon or talk, or even to consider the possibility of a whole service devoted to the theme of dementia. There are many ways to go about this. Recently I was part of a group planning and delivering an all-age 'service of the word' in a thriving village church whose members wanted to explore the idea of becoming more dementia-friendly. We chose the theme of treasure—something that appeals particularly to the young—and used R.S. Thomas' poem 'The Bright Field'[4] as the framework. This poem expresses the writer's insight that the present moment is a treasure we easily miss in our obsession with the past and the future. It alludes to two biblical stories: Moses and the burning bush, and Jesus' teaching on the treasure in the field and the pearl of great price. So our Old Testament reading was Exodus 2:23—3:7, which emphasises that the burning bush appears because God has heard the cries of his people and is responding to their suffering. Our New Testament reading was Matthew 13:44–46.

Instead of a sermon, we had a reading of the poem combined with some music, and then I invited members of the congregation, young and old, to come to the front and share 'treasures'. (The previous week I had primed them by talking about the concept of memory boxes in a slot during the regular morning worship.) This was a very moving part of the service as some people had lost a loved one to dementia and carried mementoes of them with them all the time. One lady shared her spectacle case, which she had made from a tie belonging to her deceased husband (he apparently had a prized collection). 'He is always with me,' she said. Others shared mementoes of children or significant times in their lives. A couple of children had brought toys. The degree of openness and vulnerability yet also great joy in sharing was remarkable, and after the service people reflected that they had very quickly got to know each other in a new way.

At the end of the sharing I said a prayer of blessing on the treasures, whether or not they had been shared publicly. Then I reminded the congregation that the reading from Exodus tells us God hears us when we cry out to him in our suffering. I added that, while memories are treasures, God comes to us here and now even when our memories fail. These encounters with the living God in the present moment are also to be treasured.

The prayers were led by the children, expressed in the language of remembering those for whom we pray, and using a large treasure chest into which the written prayers were placed. The hymns included 'Tell me the old, old story', 'Lord, for the years', and 'Dear Lord and Father of mankind'.[5]

All of this enabled the gathered community to reflect on the issues raised by dementia in a positive and playful manner, yet had a deep theology at its heart. It has been part of that community's continuing journey to embrace a culture that is less fearful of and more open to dementia and those directly affected by it.

A way in the wilderness

Church buildings come in a variety of forms, but they can all present challenges to people with dementia and their carers. It can be difficult to see where you are going in a dimly lit space, but bright lighting can feel threatening or overstimulating. It is nice to be in a cosy, homely space but it feels constricted if your need is to walk about freely. The needs of different individuals, and even the same individual in different phases of the condition, are varied. *The key is to be flexible enough to respond on an individual basis rather than thinking there is a single blueprint for a dementia-friendly environment.*

As cognitive deficits are made worse by hearing loss, a properly functioning hearing-loop system is highly desirable. If the overall space is large it may be helpful to arrange things so there is a *natural circuit around which a restless person can walk freely* while others are sitting or standing to worship. It is also good to have a safe space—perhaps a carpeted side chapel or corner with comfortable but supportive seating—that can be a refuge *for people to be quiet and take time out as necessary*. Labelling this as 'Quiet zone' gives clarity and is something people are familiar with from quiet carriages on trains. Notice that such features of the environment are also helpful to young children and their parents, as are readily accessible toilets.

People with dementia sometimes have perceptual problems, which means they have a distorted experience of their physical environment. This is not a problem with their eyes, but with the parts of their brain that make sense of input from their eyes. For example, they may find it difficult to see the position of a cup in relation to a table, to distinguish a toilet bowl from a sink, or to work out where the toilet ends and floor and wall tiles begin. The neutral colours beloved of many interior designers are not helpful here. *Careful use of fairly bright, contrasting colours for table linen, crockery, doors, door handles, toilet seats, floors and so on can make the environment less disorientating*.

Working out the difference between the ladies' and the gents' toilets makes life too complicated; *it is better to go for unisex toilets*. These are also much more suitable when the affected person is cared for by someone of the opposite sex (as is so often the case); they can go in together without fear of embarrassment. If you are designing a washroom area from scratch, it is better to have a small number of large unisex toilets accessible to disabled people than a large number of single-sex toilets.

Any means of *marking the edges of steps, thresholds or borders between different types of flooring will make the environment less ambiguous and frightening* (strong adhesive tape of a contrasting colour will do). It is better not to use black mats as they can appear like holes in the floor. Again, this is also a feature of the experience of young children, who may avoid stepping on these areas because they are not entirely sure if they are solid and safe.

Clear signage is also important (large print on laminated sheets works well and avoids the need to obtain official permission if the signs are simply stuck on with Blu Tack instead of something more permanent). Signs should indicate the way to the toilets *and the way back* from them into the main part of the building, as finding the way back from the toilet when faced with a number of doors can be a challenge for most people, whether or not they have dementia. It is not necessary to have a lot of signs. 'Way into church', 'EXIT', 'Toilets', 'Tea and coffee' and 'Quiet zone' may be sufficient. It is also worth considering having some very clear pictures to go with the most important signs. Having said this, signage tends to help those with stable and mild cognitive problems. It may help in the early phases of dementia, and it certainly makes the environment more welcoming to all, but as dementia advances the affected individual may simply cease to notice signs.

All are welcome in this place

People who have been members of churches for many years may gradually withdraw as they become frail or experience cognitive impairment. This can be for a number of reasons: anxiety about using the toilets; fatigue; pain; confusion about the times of services; or worry that they will not know what to do. One of the most frequent and fundamental reasons is problems with transport. The person concerned may no longer be able to drive; may have difficulty in physically accessing public transport, be short of cash or have forgotten how to order a taxi; or perhaps the carer can no longer be the driver because the affected individual needs to be looked after during the journey. *Offering a lift to a person who is no longer able to transport themselves to church is one of the most helpful ways of showing hospitality.* This can be done on an informal basis, as between friends, but it may be wiser to have a team of people who can offer lifts, to cover for illness and holidays, and who have some training or awareness of safeguarding issues.[6]

Sometimes people don't turn up for church events because they have simply forgotten about them. This is a particular issue for those who live alone. *Phoning to remind a person with dementia a couple of days beforehand and again on the day itself may feel intrusive but is probably the lesser of two evils*—the other one being to increase isolation by not reaching out. Again, a team could take it in turns to do this. The principle also applies to keeping in social contact more generally. The person with dementia may show less initiative about getting in touch, but that doesn't necessarily mean he doesn't care. The normal turn-taking that goes on in social relationships may have to be modified, with others generally making the first move.

Once through the church door, the quality of welcome is crucial. *It helps if the welcome team wear clear name badges*, and it may be good to get into the habit of everyone who wishes making a badge for themselves at the beginning of the service, rather as people do at conferences. *It will also help if the person is greeted by name* and subtly orientated. For example, 'Hello, George. How lovely to see you. My name is Joanna and we met last time you were here at church a couple of weeks back. Isn't the weather warm for April?'

Obviously this depends on the members of the welcome team being primed and having some awareness of how to communicate with people with dementia. *It is a good idea for members of the pastoral teams in churches to undergo some training in dementia awareness, and if possible to be 'dementia friends'.*[7] This can be done in a short training session or by watching a video online. This will not make them experts on dementia but it will, more importantly, give them confidence in drawing alongside someone with dementia. They will understand the principles of going with the flow; making eye contact; allowing sufficient time for the person to process what has been said and then respond; and not asking direct questions or contradicting the person.

It is actually quite difficult to make small talk without asking direct questions such as 'How are the grandchildren?' 'Have you been on holiday yet?' 'Did you have a nice Christmas?' or even 'How are you?' If we try to avoid this by focusing on the immediate environment, this can go wrong because the person with dementia may see it differently; we may point out a beautiful stained-glass window, but he may focus on the bars across it that remind him of his time as a prisoner of war. Often we may need simply to be silent. This may go against the grain, as we are used to connecting with people by making conversation, and it may seem rude to say little or nothing. But it is part of the skill set for being hospitable to the person with dementia. A light touch of the hand can communicate warmth quite effectively instead.

One of the things that can happen in dementia is the emergence of something known technically as emotionalism. I studied this as part of my PhD research, and it can be described as essentially an increased readiness to cry or (less commonly) to laugh resulting from conditions affecting the brain.[8] This can be hugely embarrassing for the affected individual and quite upsetting for others in the vicinity. Basically, the sorts of things that make most of us a little dewy-eyed can evoke full-blown weeping or hysterical laughter in the person with dementia. This is particularly problematic if a person is prone to laughing at sad occasions, when he certainly doesn't feel amused. People who cry too readily or excessively often do feel somewhat sad, but they don't experience the level of distress we would normally associate with outbursts of weeping. It is more an extreme form of sentimentality evoked by such things as romantic films, pictures of grandchildren, acts of kindness, poetry, music or prayers. In my research I found that people with this condition felt very isolated because others tended to avoid talking to them 'for fear of upsetting them'.

This is very important because church services (especially those involving children) are prone to making us sentimental, as are kind overtures by those around us. *If a person with dementia regularly weeps when she attends church, do not assume this is because she doesn't want to be there, or rush to suggest she stays away. Instead, try to find out a bit more about what is going on.*

Through whom we have access

Suitable transport is the first step towards accessing church, but difficulties in getting to the place of worship at the right time and on the right day are only the first in a series of potential barriers to participating in the gathered faith community. If the individual has difficulty negotiating steps or is a wheelchair user, then level access or a temporary ramp need to be in place. Pathways through churchyards can be slippery or, conversely, if they are gravelled, offer too much resistance to wheelchairs. They may not be well lit, making winter services occasions of real or perceived danger. They may simply be too long; contrary to the public stereotype, many people with physical disabilities are not wheelchair users but can only walk short distances slowly. Strategically placed benches along the path can help here. *Having a member of the welcome team at the gate rather than the door, prepared to direct or accompany as necessary, could be transformative.*

Once inside, access to worship needs to be considered. Does the individual need help to find spectacles or switch on a hearing aid? For a service of Holy Communion, is the altar in the most easily accessible place, or does coming forward to receive the elements involve a long and hazardous walk in which stone steps are to be negotiated? The assumption in such cases is that Communion can be taken to 'the frail' in their seats, but it may be better to move the altar. *For many people the walk forward to receive Communion is part of their devotions, and they may not want to be singled out as having special needs.* If the altar can't be moved, a more radical idea might be to have some services where Communion is brought to all members of the congregation in their seats to give a sense of solidarity with those who cannot get up and come forward.

A church may be so physically inhospitable to people with physical and cognitive disabilities that special services may need to be held in a comfortable location such as a church hall or parish room. This often happens naturally, with quieter midweek services in a more homely environment being favoured by people affected by dementia. This is good, but does not mean the main Sunday congregation is released from its requirement to make worship as accessible as possible. The danger is that the weekday service will be seen as 'other' and peripheral to the main Sunday event, as will the people who attend it. *Even if one particular service is favoured by people affected by dementia because of its location, noise levels or time, this should not be seen as the 'service for people with dementia' or even the 'dementia-friendly service'.* Everyone with dementia is different, and lumping them together according to just one aspect of their life simply stigmatises and separates them.

There are some general considerations in designing worship that will be accessible and meaningful for people with dementia. First, *it is good to use forms of words with which they are familiar*; getting the words wrong is frustrating and humiliating. For the current generation this means using the older form of the Lord's Prayer and, for Anglicans, including prayers from the old version of *The Book of Common Prayer*. Where traditional hymns are to be sung, it is better to avoid versions that have been updated by using inclusive language (these are often clumsy and annoying to everybody anyway). Many older people are also familiar with worship songs, and this will increasingly become the case, so these shouldn't be rejected out of hand. It is not necessary to tailor the whole content of a Sunday service to the special needs of people with dementia. Including a number of basic landmarks will be sufficient to make them feel at home, and you can't please all of the people all of the time anyway; moaning about newfangled gimmicks may be quite a normal part of post-worship conversations.

Even if your church projects the words of the service on to a screen, *it is good for people with dementia to have something in their hand to read or to look at*, so consider having some printed versions. If you use a complicated service booklet with lots of options and 'go to page 6'-type statements, make a special simplified service booklet. Use a large font size (sans serif 14–16 point is best).

Print out the Bible readings. People who have sensory or cognitive problems benefit from being able to hear *and* see what is being read (and some readers do not project their voices properly). You may wish to consider having some readings from the old King James Version (KJV). Young people are surprisingly receptive to this, and everyone appreciates its poetry. Perhaps you could have one reading from *The Message Remix*[9] and one from the KJV. Both have their own freshness. However, it is always important to check which version of the Bible has been most familiar to the affected individual; for example, some older people have grown up with the Good News Bible.

Finally, remember that *some people may start coming to church for the first time after a diagnosis of dementia. Don't make assumptions about their familiarity with the Christian faith*. Instead try to find out what or whom they are seeking and try to support them in their search. Dementia may actually be an occasion for flowering of faith.

Further reading

Susan H. McFadden and John T. McFadden, *Aging Together: Dementia, friendship and flourishing communities* (Johns Hopkins University Press, 2011).

Margaret Goodall and Gaynor Hammond, *Growing Dementia-Friendly Churches: A practical guide* (Christians on Ageing and MHA, 2014): www.mha.org.uk/files/3814/0931/8295/Growing_Dementia_Friendly_Churches.pdf

Notes

1   S.H. McFadden and J.T. McFadden, *Aging Together: Dementia, friendship and flourishing communities* (Johns Hopkins University Press, 2011), p. 147.

2   Z.V. Segal, J.M.G. Williams and J.D. Teasdale, *Mindfulness-Based Cognitive Therapy for Depression* (Guilford, 2012), p. 292.

3   www.cofe-worcester.org.uk/news/2016/04/28/dementia-awareness-week

4   R.S. Thomas, 'The Bright Field', *Laboratories of the Spirit* (Macmillan, 1975).

5   'Tell me the old, old story' (1866), Arabella Catherine Hankey; 'Lord, for the years' (1969), Timothy Dudley-Smith; 'Dear Lord and Father of mankind' (1872), John Greenleaf Whittier, adapted into a hymn by William Garrett Horder in 1884.

6   These will be discussed in detail in Chapter 14.

7   This is an initiative of the Alzheimer's Society: www.dementiafriends.org.uk

8   J. Collicutt McGrath, 'A study of emotionalism in patients undergoing rehabilitation following severe acquired brain injury', *Behavioural Neurology,* 12 (2000), pp. 201–7.

9   E.H. Peterson, *The Message Remix: The Bible in contemporary language* (NavPress, 2004).

Chapter 11

Real belonging

It is good for churches to be hospitable to people with dementia, but we need to think through what this means quite carefully. It is not as if the Church is over here and people with dementia are over there waiting to be invited in. People with dementia are *already* part of the Church and have a stake in it. There is a sense in which they are welcoming themselves. This is reminiscent of a scene from David Lean's 1966 film *Doctor Zhivago*,[1] in which the eponymous hero attempts to welcome people into his home only to be told in no uncertain terms by a Communist Party official, 'It is not for *you* to welcome *us*.' The point is that the house belongs to the state; it is not Zhivago's personal domain.

This is put rather well by Anne Basting, who takes the image of picking up stitches in lives that have become unravelled in an interesting direction. After affirming that people with dementia need to be re-membered by 'creating a net of social memory around' them, she goes on to say, 'This doesn't mean that we should visit people more. This means that people with memory loss need to be reknit into the fabric of our lives.'[2]

We are not knitting them together; we *all* 'must grow up in every way into him who is the head, into Christ, from whom the whole body, joined and knit together by every ligament with which it is equipped, as each part is working properly, promotes the body's growth in building itself up in love' (Ephesians 4:15–16). *A dementia-friendly church goes beyond welcome. It recognises that people with dementia are more than guests—they are members of the people of God.* This is a community of mutual obligation from which people with dementia can benefit and to which they can contribute.

Benefiting from community life

The life of a church goes beyond Sunday worship, both through its going out to connect with the wider community of which it is part, and through any gatherings that take place on its premises during the week. At least some of these activities could be designed to be particularly appropriate for people in various phases of dementia, especially the early to middle phases, in which conventional forms of social interaction are still much appreciated.

I know of one church that, once a month, organises a lunch specifically for people with dementia and their carers. As many as 80 people attend, paying a small charge to cover costs. The cooking and serving are done by volunteers. As well as lunch, there is a short talk on a topic of interest and a raffle. The opportunity for carers to socialise is especially appreciated, and there has been at least one marriage of people who originally met there as carers of their respective spouses but later became widowed. Of course, this sort of lunch club could be offered by any community group, but it may be that a church feels it has the people power and resources to take a lead in this area.

Nevertheless, the norm is likely to be more modest and less specialist. Many churches offer lunch clubs and coffee mornings that, while not targeting people with dementia, provide an accepting space in which to enjoy the company of others. These can become more intentionally dementia-friendly if the regular helpers undergo some dementia-awareness training. It may be possible for the church to offer somewhere for carers to have a break while their loved ones are enjoying lunch. This space could be used for prayer and reflection, or for experiencing some pampering such as a massage or manicure. This obviously requires more planning and resources, both in providing something appropriate for carers, and also in ensuring that safeguarding requirements are met, because helpers will effectively become responsible for vulnerable adults if carers are in another part of the building.

Apart from general socialisation, there are some specific activities that are enjoyable and stimulating for people with dementia. These might be part of a lunch club or coffee morning, but could stand alone. One example is group singing. This can either be a traditional sing-song or a more focused piece of choral singing. The Alzheimer's Society has developed a version of this called Singing for the Brain.[3] This is a group activity for people with dementia and their carers, with a clear structure and routine that involves some movement while seated and some breathing exercises. There are several reasons why this might be a good thing to do. As we have seen, musical perception appears to be preserved for longer than other faculties in many types of dementia; exercise of the upper body and more effective breathing are likely to increase blood oxygenation and induce endorphin release, which in turn encourage a sense of well-being; it is an activity that simply involves being in the present; it is communal and so should reduce isolation; it gives an opportunity for vocal articulation to people who may be largely silent. Research studies have shown that, even when people's general abilities are declining, this activity may enable their quality of life to remain stable.[4] The most potent factor may be the sense of corporate belonging that is engendered by the experience, so it might perhaps be more aptly named 'Singing for the Body'.

> Singing for the Brain… is [a] collective endeavour… it is the overall effect that is unique about the experience. The holistic, tangible nature of group singing depends on the survival of channels of musical and social intelligence on which participation depends. These seem to outlive the verbal and logical domains that so easily represent the means by which we label people as active, social beings.[5]

An exciting initiative based in Cardiff is the Forget-me-Not Chorus, which originally developed under the umbrella of the Welsh National Opera and the local branch of the Alzheimer's Society. This group uses a range of artistic media to work creatively with people affected by dementia. It has a performance-based facet, with some members taking part in concerts.

The success of these initiatives gives an indication of the great potential of music in general, and singing in particular, as a way into community participation and self-expression for people with dementia. For some people, music has a spiritual dimension, and this sort of singing may for them be a form of worship. Churches are strongly associated with music and often have good musical resources. They are a natural venue for singing groups of all kinds, including groups for adults with special needs.

Various forms of reminiscence are also particularly suitable for people with dementia. Activities might include watching films and newsreels; listening to music; or looking at postcards, newspapers or other artefacts. All these will date from times during the early life of group members. Local museums can be very helpful in providing appropriate materials, and it is worth getting in touch with them anyway because some will actually come and run a reminiscence session for you. It is also of course possible to incorporate aspects of the church building itself, such as memorial windows, as a focus for reminiscence. These sorts of sessions are essentially nostalgia trips, and they can be enjoyed by anyone whether or not they have dementia. The old find it enjoyable and stimulating to look back; the young are curious to know how things used to be. Encountering artefacts from the past can be a great stimulus to storytelling, and could perhaps be a way into some group work on personal autobiographies or making memory boxes. Reminiscence sessions might happen at regular intervals, or perhaps be part of a more intensive 'holiday at home'[6] event that takes place over a single week during the summer.

This is a little different from the spiritual reminiscence described in Chapter 9, which is a more specialist spiritual intervention with a therapeutic feel focused specifically on individuals living with dementia, and which requires facilitators who are skilled in pastoral care. Both types of reminiscence activity are possible in a church setting, and the decision of which to pursue will depend on the nature of the pastoral care team, the number of volunteers available and the preferences and needs of potential group members.

The important thing is not to let the excellent be the enemy of the good. Excellent initiatives should be inspiring not intimidating. You may not be able to offer full-blown Singing for the Brain sessions, but don't let that stop you organising a sing-along. You may not be qualified in reminiscence therapy, but don't let that stop you making some memory boxes. Like the woman who anointed Jesus at Bethany (Mark 14:8), you should do what you can and what fits your situation.

Contributing to the life of the community

Somebody once said that you belong to a community if they miss you when you're not there. This is why very big and apparently successful churches can feel alienating: it doesn't seem as if your presence makes a difference. This is also the experience of people who are always on the receiving end of care. It's lovely to be cared for, but it's even more lovely to be needed. We are made to give as well as to take. Even though it's all about God (p. 84), God graciously chooses to work *with* us, and when he became incarnate in Jesus he chose to need human beings.[7]

Being needed gives our life purpose and meaning—even if the only one who needs us is the cat. It also gives a sense of belonging, because human communities do not tolerate perceived freeloaders.[8] Conversely, if we don't feel as if our community needs us we will feel useless to it, and it's only a short step from this to feeling worthless in an absolute sense. For older people who are losing their physical and cognitive abilities, this may be expressed in the vocabulary of 'burden' and the sentiment that it would be better all-round if they were dead.

People in the early to middle phases of dementia still have a lot to give to their communities in practical terms, but they will need to be supported if their potential is to be realised. Gaynor Hammond, one of the authors of *Growing Dementia-Friendly Churches*, gives examples of people who are beginning to fail at tasks being 'retired with dignity' from the welcome team or coffee rota, when it would have been so much better if they had continued with appropriate support from a buddy.[9] This is because they are not simply carrying out a function that could be done more efficiently by others; they are bringing something of themselves to the task and the community. Where possible, this unique contribution should be enabled as long as they wish it.

It may be that a shift in activity is appropriate. A person who has carried out a duty for the community that requires a lot of standing and remembering may find a new lease of life by, for example, joining the team knitting squares to be made up as blankets to be sent to refugee camps. Such *shifts of role are made a lot easier if it is the pattern in the church as a whole for people to move between posts, with no 'jobs for life'.* This is an especially good idea for formal administrative positions, and can actually make these roles easier to fill as people are more likely to volunteer if they don't think they will end up being stuck with them. Doing things in pairs is a great confidence builder, allows for cover if one party is unwell or needs to be away (as is increasingly the case with current lifestyles), and is in line with the teaching of Jesus (Mark 6:7; Luke 10:1).

Older people, including those with dementia, are often good at relating to children and young people, yet many churches keep children and older people apart. This is deeply regrettable because

> church at its best is one of the few social gatherings where you can find representatives of every age, from the baby in arms to a nonagenarian in a wheelchair. A healthy church community is surely one that embraces all-age diversity and celebrates God-given difference, and where there is a dynamic encounter of like with unlike. The perspective of someone who has lived through war in the last century or the sexual revolution of the 1960s may be very different from that of a young 21st-century digital native, but each needs the other to enrich lives for good, and most assuredly for growing in faith.[10]

As has already been noted, young people like to hear stories of times gone by from people who were actually there. Older people are invigorated by the freshness, energy and can-do attitude of young people. People with dementia may still be able to pass on practical skills such as knitting, whittling, baking or fishing to the young. People with more advanced dementia may still react with joy to the touch of a baby. The physical skill of holding a baby seems to be retained for a very long time, and the opportunity to do so (supervised) can give a great sense of mastery. I know of one woman with advanced dementia who spoke very little, but on seeing a small child about to go into the garden of her care facility suddenly became alert and said, 'She'll need a cardigan on.' Consider bringing a preschool group and a group of older people together. Both enjoy singing, and it's possible to construct games using soft balls, beanbags and a play parachute, which can be fun for all. *If run well*, with enough helpers, a clear structure and a short session length, these initiatives can be amazingly successful. The preschoolers learn to relate naturally to older people, and even people with quite advanced dementia can contribute because they often know the words to nursery rhymes that everyone else has forgotten. All find it life-giving.

People affected by dementia also need to continue their involvement with the worship and governance of their church at a level appropriate to their wishes and abilities. Church members can support carers' continued involvement by offering to be with their loved ones, so they can attend meetings or services. The wishes and opinions of people with dementia can and should be sought directly (not simply by asking their carers). However, this can be hugely challenging,[11] and more is often learnt through attending carefully to their behaviour (looking to see when they appear relaxed and joyful as opposed to tense or agitated) and reflecting on the reasons for it. Key considerations are the level of stimulation; the demands made by the situation; temperature and lighting; the physical features of the environment; and whether their physiological needs for food, drink and the toilet are being met. For example, a person with dementia may really want to be part of a midweek service, but if there isn't a chance to visit the loo before it begins she may appear restless and distracted throughout. It is important to be able to read behaviour in order to work out the wishes of a person with dementia.

Finally, the spiritual insights of people with dementia need to be valued, attended to and received. Ways of celebrating the contribution of people affected by dementia will be explored in Chapter 12. A first step towards this is to understand and acknowledge that they have continuing spiritual needs that should be taken seriously.

Going on growing

We grow in many ways throughout our lives. Part of the philosophy of 'it is good for us to be here' is that, even in the context of dementia, we can continue to grow as human beings, particularly in our spiritual lives. Researchers in human development have identified three phases of human growth: the early phase, which is dominated by physical growth and increasing capacities; the middle phase, which is dominated by maintenance of fairly stable capacities; and the third phase, which is dominated by the regulation of loss—managing reduced capacities. Yet even in this third phase, there is still opportunity for growth in focused areas against the backdrop of significant losses.[12] In dementia the losses are massive, but we should not assume this means growth is impossible.

A retired parish priest of my acquaintance, who was physically frail and residing in a care home, once spoke to me of the frustrations of his situation. His body was imposing heavy restrictions on him, yet he still felt called to be an active minister of the gospel. He likened it to the circumstances of the apostle Paul, who was able to preach the gospel effectively even though he was in chains (Philippians 1:12–13). Paul continued to press on (Philippians 3:13–14), even in the context of great restriction and limitation. This notion of pressing on even when imprisoned by physical and cognitive disabilities is, I think, deeply encouraging. It also connects back with the tradition considered in Chapter 6 of Jesus going out of his way to make a proclamation to the spirits in prison.

So, how can people with dementia go on growing in Christ? We have already seen that meditative or silent prayer offers opportunities for spiritual nourishment when language has failed, and that objects and symbols can be important. *Prayer walks and labyrinths may be helpful for those who find sitting still difficult.* Praying on the move is good, but so is praying at stations along the way. There are lots of ideas around for constructing prayer stations that engage all the senses. A particularly successful initiative is Prayer Spaces in Schools,[13] which, as its name suggests, is aimed at children and young people. Each set-up consists of a number of prayer stations at which participants are invited to carry out an activity as a prayer. Sometimes specific prayer requests are voiced as part of the activity. Sometimes the station is contemplative, involving something such as looking at a bubble tube or a lava lamp and raising prayers upwards; sometimes it is active, involving, for example, making human figures from pipe cleaners as a way of expressing human fellowship. The stations are arranged according to existential themes such as identity, peace and questions. While basically Christian, they are not overtly religious and take an open-ended approach. This means they can be used by children and young people of all faiths and none.

These sorts of stations can be enjoyed by people of all ages. I have been involved in using a prayer-space approach at a county-council-run centre for vulnerable older people. The activities needed modification to be at table height, but otherwise were very similar to those in a normal Prayer Spaces in Schools set-up. We included planting bulbs in little pots to give to grandchildren to express hope in the coming generations; a tree of knowledge on to which we hung cards with 'wise words you would like to tell young people today'; and contemplation of a bubble tube to aid relaxation and peacefulness. We found that all the stations elicited reminiscences from the older people who participated.

The devotional life of some people includes reading the Bible or reciting it from memory. Memories of specific Bible passages are usually near the bottom of the airing cupboard, so to speak, and also based strongly on implicit procedural memory, so are likely to be preserved for some time. In a similar way, some prayers are overlearnt in certain subcultures. For most indigenous Britons over the age of 60 this is currently the case for the old version of the Lord's Prayer and Psalm 23, but this may change with future generations. Some prayers from childhood are also well remembered and loved.

> *Thank you for the world so sweet;*
> *Thank you for the food we eat;*
> *Thank you for the birds that sing;*
> *Thank you, God, for everything.*[14]

I have found that Ladybird books of prayers and Bible stories from the 1950s and 60s are appreciated as part of reminiscence work with people aged 60 and above. While there is a danger that looking at children's books can be seen as a patronising activity, it can also be framed as pleasurable browsing through vintage artefacts. The memories may be of having used these books as a teacher or parent rather than as a child. There is also a series of beautifully illustrated books published by Pictures to Share,[15] designed specifically for people with dementia and other conditions affecting thought and language. These cover all aspects of life, but there is one specifically devoted to spiritual themes called *Strength for the Journey*.[16]

If daily devotional Bible reading has been part of a person's lifelong practice, this can be supported. Some publishers produce material specifically targeted at people in the early to middle stages of dementia.[17] However, it is essential that Bible reading is not reduced to dementia-driven content. It should continue to cover the full range of praise and lament, story and poetry, assurance and mystery. There will come a point when it is more helpful for a carer to read a short passage in a familiar translation to the affected individual, rather than expecting her to read it herself. Given that feelings about a passage will be retained longer than its content, these brief encounters should end on a peaceful note. It may be helpful if this always takes the same form, such as 'The grace of the Lord Jesus Christ, the love of God, and the fellowship of the Holy Spirit be with us both evermore' (2 Corinthians 13:13, GNT, altered), or 'The Lord bless you and keep you; the Lord make his face to shine upon you, and be gracious to you; the Lord lift up his countenance upon you, and give you peace' (Numbers 6:24–26).

Spirituality involves transcendence—going beyond ourselves. Many of the activities suggested in this chapter support this process through enabling prayer, engagement with scripture and connection with others. Lament, where appropriate, can be a significant part of this process, and in Chapter 9 the importance of receiving the distress of people affected by dementia was emphasised. But there is a counterpoint to this. Positive emotion takes us out of ourselves so that we start to be concerned with others. This principle is called 'broaden and build'.[18] *We all need to experience some happiness if we are to grow spiritually.*

Here is an example recently shared with me by a dementia adviser. She had received a phone call from a man who regularly visited his mother in her residential care home. He was experiencing a good deal of grief and frustration because, by his account, his mother was in a world of her own and he could not get through to her. She kept talking about the horses that were galloping in the field outside her window. He wanted to talk to her as he had always done about his life, and especially about her granddaughters, but she just kept on about the horses, even when he reminded her that they were in the middle of a town with no horses for miles. His mother was a great horse lover and had owned horses during an earlier period of her life. The conversation then went on:

Dementia adviser: What is actually outside her window?
Caller: Oh, just a brick wall and a couple of parked cars.
Dementia adviser: Well, which would *you* rather see?

The adviser then suggested that instead of contradicting his mother, the caller should try to enter her reality and be present with her in it. Sounding rather sceptical, he agreed to give it a go. He phoned back a couple of weeks later to say that not only had he been able to have a happy conversation with his mother about her love of horses, but this also seemed to have expanded her horizon. For the first time in years she asked him how *he* was, and brought him to tears by enquiring how her granddaughters were doing.

If we can draw joy out of people—or draw people into joy—by whatever means, we are likely to find that they become more concerned for others, more fully present to them, and therefore continue to grow in the life of faith. Joy is the second fruit of the Spirit (Galatians 5:22–23), and it is central to the topic of the next chapter—celebration.

Further reading

Martyn Payne, *Messy Togetherness: Being intergenerational in Messy Church* (BRF, 2016).
Holly Catterton Allen and Christine Lawton Ross, *Intergenerational Christian Formation: Bringing the whole church together in ministry, community and worship* (IVP, 2012).
Louise Morse, *Worshipping with Dementia: Meditations, scriptures and prayers for sufferers and carers* (Monarch, 2010).
Seasons of My Soul: Conversations in the second half of life, produced by the Church of England and the Methodist Church (Methodist Publishing, 2014).

Notes

1 The film was adapted from the book of the same name: B. Pasternak, *Doctor Zhivago* (Pantheon, 1957).
2 A. Basting, *Forget Memory: Creating better lives for people with dementia* (John Hopkins University Press, 2009), p. 161.
3 www.alzheimers.org.uk/site/scripts/documents_info.php?documentID=ID=760
4 P.M. Camic, C.M. Williams and F. Meeten, 'Does a "Singing Together Group" improve the quality of life of people with a dementia and their carers? A pilot evaluation study', *Dementia,* 12 (2013), pp. 157–76.
5 N. Bannen and C. Montgomery-Smith, '"Singing for the Brain": reflections on the human capacity for music arising from a pilot study of group singing with Alzheimer's patients', *The Journal of the Royal Society for the*

Promotion of Health, 128 (2008), p. 78.

6 This initiative originated with Outlook Trust, a charity that focused on mission with older people, which produced an excellent video and handbook. The charity has now been wound up, but another good source of information is a paper written by Michael Collyer as part of the *Discovering Faith in Later Life* series produced by Church Army: www.churcharmy.org.uk/Publisher/File.aspx?ID=138315

7 For more on this see J. Collicutt, *Jesus and the Gospel Women* (SPCK, 2009), pp. 128–32.

8 L. Cosmides and J. Tooby, 'Cognitive adaptation for social exchange'. In J.H. Barkow, L. Cosmides and J. Tooby (eds), *The Adapted Mind: Evolutionary psychology and the generation of culture* (Oxford University Press, 1992), pp. 163–228.

9 M. Goodall and G. Hammond, *Growing Dementia-Friendly Churches: A practical guide* (Christians on Ageing and MHA, 2014), pp. 9–10: www.mha.org.uk/files/3814/0931/8295/Growing_Dementia_Friendly_Churches.pdf

10 J. Collicutt and M. Payne, 'The ageless kingdom of God', *Church Times* (11 December 2015).

11 C. Bamford, 'Successes and challenges in using focus groups with older people with dementia'. In H. Wilkinson (ed.), *The Perspectives of People with Dementia: Research methods and motivations* (Jessica Kingsley, 2001), pp. 139–64.

12 P.B. Baltes, U.M. Staudinger and U. Lindenberger, 'Lifespan psychology: Theory and application to intellectual functioning', *Annual Review of Psychology,* 50 (1999), pp. 471–507.

13 www.prayerspacesinschools.com

14 'A Child's Grace' by E. Rutter Leatham.

15 www.picturestoshare.co.uk

16 H.J. Bate and M. Forster (eds), *Strength for the Journey* (Pictures to Share, 2015).

17 Scripture Union produces three workbooks under the umbrella title *Being with God: A Bible and prayer guide for people with dementia.*

18 B.L. Fredrickson, 'The broaden-and-build theory of positive emotions', *Philosophical Transactions of the Royal Society B: Biological Sciences,* 359 (2004), pp. 1367–78.

Chapter 12

Celebration

There is much to be lamented about dementia, but there are also some things to be celebrated. To celebrate certain elements of dementia is not to say it's an experience we would wish on ourselves or our loved ones—and most of us wouldn't wish it on our worst enemies either. Yet this is also true when it comes to celebrating what Jesus achieved through the cross. Jesus did not seek out the way of the cross; in fact, he actively sought alternatives. But when he realised it had to be, he entered into it fully. Not only that, he also explained again and again to his followers that the way to life and light is through darkness and death.

Whether or not one accepts this radical and paradoxical theology of the cross (and many Christians, even, find it deeply unpalatable), it seems clear there are some truths learnt, some virtues attained, some strengths gained only through facing adversity. This is well summed up in Nietzsche's famous saying, 'What doesn't kill me makes me stronger.'[1] Psychologists refer to this experience as post-traumatic growth[2] and have found it to be multifaceted, displaying elements of wisdom, resilience and spiritual maturity; increased intimacy with others going through the same thing; and a greater appreciation of life as a gift. It seems this sort of growth can take place in people who care for a loved one with dementia,[3] and this may be even more marked in people of faith.[4]

One key aspect of coming through adversity well—not just surviving, but growing as a human being—is the opportunity to bear witness. Here we come back to the way of the cross, because the Greek word in the New Testament that is translated 'to bear witness' is *martureō*, from which we get the English word 'martyr'. If we are to help people facing difficult situations, we need to hear, and sometimes record, their stories. These are narrative in form, but in this context they are more than narratives; they are *testimonies*. It is in the process of constructing the testimony that the teller makes sense and comes to some sort of peace, the hearers are enlightened and the community is enriched.

A wonderful collection of stories from older people has been gathered by a team led by Keith Albans and Malcolm Johnson in a volume entitled *God, Me and Being Very Old*. It is full of wisdom, poignancy and humour. Above all it celebrates the spiritual gains that can be made in later life, even in the context of suffering and loss. One of the storytellers is 89-year-old Robert, who cared for his wife, Hazel, who had dementia, for several years until her death. This period is described as 'exhausting and traumatic'. Yet 'he really believes that God was his strength and support during those difficult days'.[5]

A dementia-friendly church is one that is prepared to acknowledge and celebrate some of these 'treasures of darkness', while at the same time recognising that the darkness can be very dark indeed. This attitude rests on the foundation that 'The light shines in the darkness, and the darkness did not overcome it' (John 1:5). In this chapter we look at some aspects of dementia that can be celebrated, and we begin with the love and care that people with dementia often receive from others.

Celebrating caregiving

Since 2001 the national census has asked people to report the amount of time they give to looking after, helping or supporting family members, friends or neighbours because of 'long-term physical or mental ill-health, or disability, or problems related to old age'. The results have revealed the extent of informal, unpaid care that takes place in the UK, and the fact that a disproportionate amount of this care is provided by people over 65.[6] This is perhaps surprising to those of us who think of older people as exclusively the recipients of care.

Of course, many older carers are caring for other older people. The most common scenarios are an older person caring for an even older parent, or an older person caring for a spouse who may be somewhat older. But older people may also be primary carers for their own children (as in the case of a relatively fit 85-year-old mother caring for her 65-year-old son who has dementia) or their grandchildren. This massive group of people is largely invisible. Indeed, a recent Age UK campaign for greater recognition of older people who give care was entitled 'Invisible but Invaluable'.[7] The invaluable bit is important: older carers save the nation millions of pounds through their unpaid service, and by the fact that they tend not to take up all the monetary benefits to which they are entitled.[8] This may be because they have difficulty negotiating the benefits system, but more fundamentally because they don't identify with the label 'carer'; they see what they are doing as a natural part of a loving relationship.

Not all these people are caring for someone with dementia, and not all carers of people with dementia are old or unpaid. There are reported (worrying) cases of grandchildren and other young people being the main carer for a person with dementia.[9] There are also obviously carers who are paid and trained volunteers. Despite this diversity, *there are some issues that are common to all types and conditions of carers. They involve personal sacrifice in the areas of money, health, social connection and social recognition.*

There are the financial costs of caregiving—the lost income from giving up work or taking a low-paid job. All caregiving is potentially detrimental to health and well-being,[10] but caring for someone with dementia is particularly emotionally demanding because of the strain placed on the relationship.[11] This increases the risk of abuse by either party.[12] Social isolation is an issue for paid carers who work antisocial hours. It is an even greater issue for family members, who can have difficulty taking a break from the caring role because of unavailability of respite services and transport, or guilt and worry at leaving their loved one. As we have seen, caregiving is often under-recognised and undervalued. Full-time carers may in addition feel a loss of independence and identity beyond the caring role (something also experienced by parents caring full-time for small children).

There are, however, some joys that come with being a carer, especially if this is perceived and recognised as a vocation. There can be great pride in caring well for loved ones, enabling them to remain in familiar and comfortable surroundings or live out their last days well. There can be moments of love and closeness, even with a person with advanced dementia. There can be growth in skill and wisdom. And, of course, there is that important sense of being needed.

There are a number of ways that church communities can recognise and respond to the needs of carers beyond providing short-term relief (e.g. cover for a hospital appointment) and supporting longer periods of respite. When a carer feels he is losing touch with the church community, a midweek service, fellowship group or church meeting might be relocated to his home, and, if necessary, a volunteer provided to be with the person who is cared for. *It is also desirable to enable carers to continue in a ministry beyond that of hands-on care.* One way of doing this is to invite a person whose main role is caregiving to address a meeting (small or large) on some aspect of life or ministry in which she has gifts, experience and wisdom. This might relate to what she has learnt through caregiving, or it may be something completely different that is life-giving for her and her listeners.

A service of celebration

Carers Week is held annually in early summer across the UK. Materials and information to support community initiatives with carers are produced and promoted during this period.[13] As part of this, or independently at another time, *a church could host a special event and/or a service of celebration and gratitude for all who give care.* This sort of service will take some planning. The aims are likely to include acknowledging and celebrating the vocation of people who give care; educating the church and wider community about the contribution of carers; setting aside a dedicated time for carers to worship unencumbered by their usual duties; offering a time of refreshment; and building informal support networks in the church and wider communities.

It may be possible to design a service at which both carer and cared-for feel comfortable. Alternatively (and this is easier) it might focus exclusively on carers. However, even in this sort of service, the reciprocal nature of the caregiving relationship should be acknowledged. Carers often talk of the unexpected gifts they receive from the person for whom they care (though for some it can feel largely thankless, so diversity of experience should be recognised).

The timing of the service is important, and will depend on the needs of the people concerned. For example, if many of the cared-for attend day-care or education centres, then a service that fits in with drop-off and pick-up times would work well. This is likely to be midweek between 11.00 am and 2.00 pm. On the other hand, many people are cared for full-time at home; their carers would need enough notice to arrange cover, or to be offered the opportunity to bring the cared-for person with them if appropriate. This will often have implications for transport, which should be factored in, and the building should be as hospitable as possible to the affected person, as outlined in Chapter 10, including a place for individuals to sit if they are not taking part in the service, and enough helpers to spend time with them.

Actually tracking down carers to invite may be a challenge because, as we have seen, much caregiving is invisible. In addition to the usual ways of advertising services, it is worth contacting the family members who reside with people who receive regular home communion, and leaving invitations in GP surgeries. (GPs have a responsibility to identify informal carers as part of the government's Carers Strategy.[14]) *Professional carers employed by local agencies or residential care facilities may also appreciate an invitation to a service of celebration. Their work needs more public recognition.*

The provision of tea, coffee (or even fizz) and cake after the service adds to the sense of celebration and affirmation. Inviting attendees to fill in cards so they can be contacted about further events would also help them feel more connected with the church.

Below is an example of a simple weekday Anglican service in celebration of older carers that I have used, and which was much appreciated by those who attended. It includes anointing with oil as a mark of both healing carer strain and recognition of caregiving as a high vocation.

— PREPARATION —

Welcome and opening prayer:

God of love and care—who chose Abraham and Sarah to care for Isaac in their old age, and Zechariah and Elizabeth to care for John in their old age; whose servants Simeon and Anna watched for the fulfilment of your kingdom and called down blessings on your Son—we give you thanks for the tender love and service of all older people who give care. This is so often a quiet and private ministry, but nothing is unseen by you. Give your church the eyes to see it, a heart to celebrate it and hands ready to help. We ask this in the name of him who gave his life for us, your Son, Jesus Christ. **Amen**

Hymn or song

The collect for the day

— LITURGY OF THE WORD —

First reading: Isaiah 46:3–4

Second reading: 2 Corinthians 1:1–5

Psalm 23—a prerecorded musical setting with a brief reflection

Third reading: 1 Corinthians 12:12–27

Sharing stories

— PRAYERS —

These use the refrain *may we* **bear one another's burdens and so fulfil the law of Christ** (based on Galatians 6:2).

Father, forgive our blindness to the courage and wisdom of those among us who give care to their loved ones. Forgive our lack of imagination; forgive our tendency to act as individual organs and not as parts of an interconnected body. Confident in your forgiveness, may we

bear one another's burdens and so fulfil the law of Christ.

We give thanks for all who work to support carers, individually and through national campaigns. We particularly think of the work of Age UK and Carers UK. May we

bear one another's burdens and so fulfil the law of Christ.

We pray for those for whom we care, naming them in the quiet of our hearts… Help us to entrust them to you. We give thanks for what they are able to give us. We offer you our worries for the future. Make us ready to ask for help and support, and give us grace to receive it. May we

bear one another's burdens and so fulfil the law of Christ.

We pray for ourselves, for health and strength—physical, emotional and spiritual. Help us to lean on you; give us others to share our load. Help us to be kind to ourselves, as you have been kind to us. Above all, keep a flame of hope burning in our hearts. May we

bear one another's burdens and so fulfil the law of Christ.

We pray for your body, the Church. Bind us together in love, so that the fruits of your Spirit may flow through our lives: love, joy, peace, patience, kindness, generosity, faithfulness, gentleness and self-control. May we

bear one another's burdens and so fulfil the law of Christ.

Then conclude with the Lord's Prayer

— ANOINTING —

Hymn or song

Those who wish receive anointing on their palms

— CONCLUSION —

Hymn or song

Let us say the grace to each other:

May the grace of our Lord Jesus Christ, and the love of God, and the fellowship of the Holy Spirit, be with us all, evermore. Amen (based on 2 Corinthians 13:13)

Celebrating the gift of the present moment

At several points in this book we have noted the way that, in certain phases, dementia forces both affected individuals and those around them to be in the present. This is at once disempowering and disorientating, but it can also open the door into another way of being that has been greatly prized in all faith traditions as liberating and in some sense deeply real. The umbrella term of mindfulness refers to a whole range of practices that are, in one way or another, directed at this notion of paying attention to the present moment without wishing it were otherwise. One of these practices is mindful colouring. This may seem rather a grandiose term for the activity of crayoning, but the concept has led to the production of colouring books appropriate for adults, which can only be good news for people with dementia. There is no doubt that concentrating on colouring in is calming for many adults and children; it's just mindless enough to support mindfulness. This is a much more modest version of the spiritual peace that can be attained by writing an icon or illuminating a sacred text, but it should not be dismissed for that. Colouring in side by side, perhaps of sacred designs, is a way of intentionally being together in the present that can be enjoyed by people across the generations. Where a person with dementia no longer has the fine-motor skills to do the task, he can still participate by choosing colours. High-quality materials are worthwhile to give the activity significance and dignity.

Colouring books are the things of child's play. In part this is because of the deep absorption they can induce. Absorption is an important characteristic of play, and there are several others: doing something for its own sake rather than as a means to something else; time flying throughout; the involvement of creativity and imagination; and above all, fun. Each of these things can, in its own way, also be seen in dementia: deep absorption; 'purposeless' activity; disengagement from the normal rules of time; existing in a world of imagination; and even, sometimes, laughter and joy. Jerome Berryman, creator of Godly Play, even goes as far as describing play as the way human beings meet their creator,[15] so perhaps *one way of celebrating dementia is to take its playful aspects seriously.*

The person who has done the most work in this area is writer John Killick. For many years, Killick has promoted playful practice among people with dementia. This can involve physical games with rules; spontaneous fun; dancing (my own experience is that people with dementia have often liked to watch me dance, or to join in and dance themselves); painting and drawing; blowing bubbles; engaging with soft toys; or sharing jokes. Killick himself focuses on words, and in particular poetry.

People whose conventional language is failing often fall back on made-up words and phrases to express themselves. These can be highly apt; for example, one woman of my acquaintance described her condition as 'my forgettery'. Killick has developed a process of careful listening to the person with dementia, and he notes down poetic phrases like this from their talk. He also tries to make some sense of their story. Then he forms their words into poems—perhaps in haiku form if the utterances have been minimal; in more flowing verse for people who talk a lot. No words are added; the person's own words are simply arranged in the most powerful way. The poems are shared with the individual and a process of joint editing takes place. The person has full ownership of the poem. If agreeable, the poem may be shared with others, and several have been published.[16]

This is an inventive way of supporting the process of testimony in people with dementia—giving them a voice; but it is much more than a way of translating apparent gibberish into something more comprehensible (or if not comprehensible, then acceptable because it's poetic). Killick's method recognises the poetry inherent in the speech and thoughts of many; it points to the ineffability of the experience, which is also a feature of mysticism. It celebrates other ways of being, thinking and experiencing, even when these involve sorrow along with joy.

The thing about play is that the output isn't important; it's the process that matters. Many creative artists would say the same about their work. Nevertheless, as with art, play often produces output in the form of poems, stories, pictures and models, and these could be incorporated into the worship and physical environment of a church. *For example, instead of praying for people with dementia in public worship, why not incorporate poems or use prayers written by people with dementia? Why not use a loaf of bread baked by a group of people with dementia in a service of Holy Communion?*

Celebrating the life of a person with dementia

People with dementia eventually die. Dementia is itself a life-limiting condition because, in its late stages, the body's ability to function declines, resulting in physical weakness; on top of this, the affected person may not be willing or able to eat and drink. Often, things don't get as far as this because the affected individual succumbs to pneumonia or another infection. And, of course, just like the rest of us, people with dementia can suffer strokes and heart attacks or develop cancer.

The death trajectories of people with dementia are therefore highly variable and also unpredictable. As doctors are prepared to make a diagnosis earlier and earlier in the course of the condition, it is hard to pin down the average time between diagnosis and death. Many people live with the condition for ten or more years and, as with many older people, they can be 'at death's door' and then rally several times. This can be stressful for family members who have, over many years, been saying goodbye to the person they once knew, and who then set themselves up for the final goodbye only to find that a very frail version of that person is still with them. It is made easier if that person appears to be at peace; however, in dementia this is by no means always the case, as the quality of palliative care for this group lags behind that for the rest of the population.[17]

The overwhelming feeling when death finally comes tends, therefore, to be one of relief. If churches are to be hospitable to people who turn to them, perhaps for the first time, at this point, they need to take this sense of relief (and the guilt that sometimes goes with it) into account, and to affirm it as a normal reaction. The relief may persist at least until the funeral, or there may be a kind of numbness. This is in part because the loss is so ambiguous, and there are no clear social norms for what a person 'should' feel.

People react to the loss of a loved one differently from each other; there is no normative set of stages to be gone through. This is even more the case when the loved one has died with dementia. However, there are usually some general processes at work. The most important of these are 'placing' the deceased (physically through burial or interment of ashes, and psychologically through working out where the deceased is in your own head); and finding a way to maintain continuing bonds with him or her.[18]

The placing process seems to start before the physical death of the affected person, when relatives ask, 'Is she still in there somewhere?' or 'Where has he gone?' People often make sense of questions like these by embracing a dualism in which their loved one has departed, but his or her body still remains. The extract below is from a poem by Dick Underwood that is a popular choice for the funeral of a person with dementia:

> You didn't die just recently,
> You died some time ago.
> Although your body stayed a while,
> And didn't really know.
> For you had got Alzheimer's,
> You failed to comprehend.
> Your body went on living.
> But your mind had reached its end.
> So we've already said, 'Goodbye,'
> To the person that we knew.
> The person that we truly loved,
> The person that was 'you'.[19]

The poem goes on to describe the funeral as merely laying the body to rest. While this appears rather at odds with orthodox Christian teaching about the integration of soul and body, it is entirely understandable that people make psychological sense of dementia in this way, and this should be respected. Nevertheless, the reason these sentiments have to be asserted rather than assumed is that mourners are generally in a more ambiguous place than indicated by the words of the poem; the person who has died was at the same time their loved one and not their loved one. One man whose relative had frontotemporal dementia told me the family coped by imagining their loved one had gone and his dodgy cousin had come to stay; the husband of a lady with vascular dementia said to me, 'I care for this poor creature for the sake of my dear wife.'

For all the above reasons, my own feeling is that **the funeral of a person with dementia should not be too ambitious.** It should allow the bereaved some breathing space, while at the same time indicating closure for the period of the person's life that was marked, if not dominated, by dementia. It should meet the mourners where they are—very early in the process of making sense and re-membering their loved one—and it should emphasise that the person is now at peace. The commendation is especially significant as a way of handing over care responsibilities from the carers to God, and imaginative ways of involving them will be necessary. Images of tucking the deceased safely in for the night, or placing him or her into God's arms, give a sense of good completion, especially if agitated walking and insomnia have been part of the story. Christian funeral services are full of appropriate images of peace, rest and handing over, all of which tune into a core sense of relief; they simply need foregrounding with skill.

It is advisable to have a separate, more celebratory memorial service some weeks or months later. If done well and collaboratively, the crafting of the service is likely to help family and friends with the process of 'placing' the whole person, not just the physical body or the person as experienced in the final years. This should contribute to the development of continuing bonds. Services like these will make good use of reminiscences, formal life-story books and memory boxes. They can explore images of the life journey and go some way to reclaiming aspects of relationships that seemed to have been eroded by dementia (for example, the capacity of the affected person to be a mother to her children). More extended theological reflection than was possible in the early days following the death may take place. This may explore ideas of the deceased as on a journey, having got through the dark tunnel of dementia to a glory that lies beyond it; or of going home to be most truly him- or herself, with body, soul and spirit integrated. Images of what this might involve (digging their allotment, or doing *The Times* crossword, or calling loved ones by name) can also be explored.

Of course, many people will not want to go through two services, and a second may not be practicable, so these principles need adapting accordingly. The re-membering and celebration may need to take place during follow-up visits, or as part of an All Souls' Day celebration service, or as part of a bereavement group. *What is clear is that the processes of re-membering and placing the deceased can't be rushed and shoehorned into the funeral.*

These principles are actually applicable to bereavement across the board; the funeral is a significant milestone, but the processes that require pastoral care go on. This is an example of where a dementia-friendly church is friendly to all. It will be aware of and respond to the continuing needs of the bereaved, through reminiscing and remembering good times and bad, making sense with hindsight and joyfully celebrating the lives of their loved ones.

Further reading

John Killick, *Playfulness and Dementia: A practice guide* (Jessica Kingsley, 2012).

Keith Albans and Malcolm Johnson (eds), *God, Me and Being Very Old: Stories and spirituality in later life* (SCM, 2013).

Stephen Joseph, *What Doesn't Kill Us: The new psychology of posttraumatic growth* (Basic Books, 2011).

Alexine Crawford, *The Challenge of Caring: Bible-based reflections* (BRF, 2011).

Therese Lysaught, 'Memory, funerals and the communion of saints: growing old and practices of remembering'. In Stanley Hauwerwas, Carole Bailey Stoneking, Keith G. Meador and David Cloutier (eds), *Growing Old in Christ* (Eerdmans, 2003), pp. 267–301.

Age UK, the Alzheimer's Society and Carers UK all produce useful, practical literature for carers. For an interesting respite initiative see www.saga.co.uk/saga-charities/saga-respite-for-carers-trust.aspx

Notes

1 From the German 'Was mich nicht umbringt, macht mich stärker.' This phrase appears in Nietzsche's book *Twilight of the Idols, or, How to Philosophize with a Hammer*, which was published in 1889.

2 R.G. Tedeschi and L.G. Calhoun, *Trauma and Transformation: Growing in the aftermath of suffering* (Sage, 1995).

3 B. Leipold, C. Schacke and S. Zank, 'Personal growth and cognitive complexity in caregivers of patients with dementia', *European Journal of Ageing,* 5 (2008), pp. 203–14; N.R. Netto, J. Go Yen Ni and P. Yap, 'Growing and gaining through caring for a loved one with dementia', *Dementia,* 8 (2009), pp. 245–61.

4 J.C. Stuckey, 'Faith, aging, and dementia experiences of Christian, Jewish, and non-religious spousal caregivers and older adults', *Dementia,* 2 (2003), pp. 337–52.

5 K. Albans and M. Johnson (eds), *God, Me and Being Very Old: Stories and spirituality in later life* (SCM, 2013), pp. 94–95.

6 Around 15% of over-65s give a significant amount of care, and older carers are likely to be giving more hours of care per week than their younger counterparts. As age increases, the amount of care provided rises; across the UK there are about 8000 people aged over 90 who provide more than 50 hours of unpaid care per week. (Based on figures from the Office for National Statistics Census 2001, the General Register Office for Scotland Census 2001 and the Northern Ireland Statistics and Research Agency Census 2001.)

7 *Invisible but Invaluable: Campaigning for greater support for older carers* (Age UK, October 2010): www.ageuk.org.uk/Documents/EN-GB/Campaigns/ID9494%20Invisible%20But%20Invaluable%20Report.pdf?dtrk=true

8 Take-up is only about 10% (based on 2005 figures from the Department of Work and Pensions, and 2003 figures from the Northern Ireland Statistics and Research Agency).

9 *Young People Caring for Adults with Dementia in England: Report on NCB's survey findings and internet research* (National Children's Bureau, March 2016): www.sheffield.ac.uk/polopoly_fs/1.563454!/file/Young_people_caring_for_adults_with_dementia.pdf

10 J. Maher and H. Green, *Carers 2000: Results from the carers module of the National Household Survey 2000* (Stationery Office, 2002); L. Annerstedt, S. Elmståhl, B. Ingvad and S.M. Samuelsson, 'Family caregiving in dementia—an analysis of the caregiver's burden and the "breaking-point"

when home care becomes inadequate', *Scandinavian Journal of Public Health,* 28 (2000), pp. 23–31.

11 P. Moïse, M. Schwarzinger and M. Um, 'Dementia care in 9 OECD countries: a comparative analysis', *OECD Health Working Papers,* 13 (OECD Publishing, 2004): http://dx.doi.org/10.1787/485700737071

12 G.M. Williamson and D.R. Shaffer, 'Relationship quality and potentially harmful behaviors by spousal caregivers: how we were then, how we are now. The Family Relationships in Late Life Project', *Psychology and Aging,* 16 (2001), pp. 217–26.

13 Carers UK organises this: www.carersuk.org

14 *Recognised, Valued and Supported: Next steps for the Carers Strategy* (Department of Health, 2010). www.gov.uk/government/uploads/system/uploads/attachment_data/file/213804/dh_122393.pdf; *Carers Strategy: Second National Action Plan 2014–16* (Department of Health, 2014): www.gov.uk/government/uploads/system/uploads/attachment_data/file/368478/Carers_Strategy_-_Second_National_Action_Plan_2014_-_2016.pdf

15 J.W. Berryman, *Godly Play: An imaginative approach to religious education* (HarperSanFrancisco, 1991), p. 17.

16 J. Killick, *Dementia Diary: Poems and prose* (Hawker Publications, 2008); J. Killick, *You Are Words: Dementia poems* (Hawker Publications, 2008).

17 V. Lawrence et al., 'Dying well with dementia: qualitative examination of end-of-life care', *The British Journal of Psychiatry,* 199 (2011), pp. 417–22.

18 D. Klass, P.R. Silverman and S.L. Nickman (eds), *Continuing Bonds: New understandings of grief* (Taylor and Francis, 1996); J.W. Worden, *Grief Counseling and Grief Therapy: A handbook for the mental health practitioner* (Springer, 2008).

19 Dick Underwood, 2010: www.smashwords.com/extreader/read/88479/9/eulogy-help

Chapter 13

Connection

It is all too easy for people with dementia to become isolated. The condition itself pushes them into their own worlds and, as we have seen, society tends to forget them. This is true of society at large; it's true of local communities where people with advancing dementia are often essentially housebound or hidden behind the doors of residential units; and it's true of churches where regular attenders gradually disappear from congregational life.

In the previous three chapters we have looked at the ideas of inclusion, belonging and celebration, largely in terms of churches as gathered congregations into which people are drawn. In this chapter we look at the other aspects of church life: the presence of the church dispersed through the wider community, and the way church makes connections through networks. The principle of building community remains the same, but the shape and location of the communities are different.

Residential care homes as communities of faith

Many churches send pastoral teams into residential care homes or sheltered housing. One way of understanding their ministry is as community building—not just re-membering the residents as individuals, but re-membering a whole community. There are a number of aspects to this ministry:

- Building a community of faith in the residential setting.
- Linking it with the local church community.
- Linking it with the wider community.
- Keeping it connected with the Christian story and the communion of saints.

The first question that presents itself is 'Who are the community members in a residential facility?' Clearly the residents are members, but the community will also incorporate staff, family and friends, and other regular visitors. Both their needs and their potential as helpers should be taken into account if visits by pastoral teams are to work well.

It is essential to have good relations with the manager of the home (and this can be challenging if turnover is high). It is important to fit in with their vision and understand the practical constraints under which the home operates.Having said that, if the manager appears reluctant to accommodate pastoral visits, it is perfectly in order to point to the Care Quality Commission's requirement that 'Staff will know, understand and respond to each person's diverse cultural, gender and spiritual needs in a caring and compassionate way.'[1] The services of the pastoral visitor(s) can be framed as a positive way of helping the facility achieve compliance in this area.

It is also very helpful to form a good collaborative relationship with the activities coordinator, if there is one. It may be that the best way to deliver spiritual care is to be part of what is already happening. One of the most successful initiatives I have come across is that of a church toddler group meeting in the sitting room of a dementia care home. This was the brainchild of the activities coordinator, who sent a general appeal to all toddler groups in her area; a local church responded and they then began to work collaboratively.

A more usual approach is to organise a regular worship service in a communal area of the home. It is necessary to give some thought about who this is for. It should be for people who actually want to be there. This means it is not really appropriate to take over the residents' sitting room unless those who do not wish to participate have somewhere else to go (though sadly this can't always be avoided). Try to mark out the space as sacred in some way, perhaps with a white cloth and a candle on a table, or flowers arranged in the shape of a cross.

It is good to invite friends and relatives who would like to join in. Some care staff should remain present to attend to residents' urgent needs, and if they can be encouraged to feel part of things (if they wish) then so much the better. It is often necessary to ask direct care staff about the specific needs of individual residents, for example, 'Does he usually wear glasses?' 'Where is his hearing aid?' 'Can he swallow safely?' It may be helpful to make notes about these, especially if different members of a pastoral team visit on different occasions; it saves asking the same questions repeatedly.

Gathering residents together can take some time, so *the service should be arranged at a convenient time, and sufficient time should be allowed for the whole event*—for preparation and waiting before the service, and for additional encounters afterwards, as individuals may require one-to-one ministry of prayer or listening. When preparing the service, do not underestimate the intelligence or spiritual capacity of residents; you may be working with a mixed group, and even people with significant cognitive problems can have lucid moments. On the other hand, you will also need to be flexible enough to respond to interjections by participants; to ditch your prepared material; and to go with the flow. The unpredictability is part of what makes these visits demanding, so build in some 'decompression time' for yourself later in the day.

What form should the service take? This very much depends on the needs and desires of the residents. It may be possible to consult a representative group of residents[2] to get a better feel for this. The choice is likely to be between Holy Communion (with the bread and wine consecrated on-site or, more commonly, brought already consecrated from the local church), or a simple 'service of the word'. Whatever you choose, you should *keep it short*. Twenty minutes is about right, though some groups may tolerate half an hour. Use a disposable or laminated order of service and give a copy to everyone who wants it; it can be reassuring to hold even for those who can't or don't actually read it. The material should be printed in a large, clear font with perhaps a picture or two, ideally all on one side.

It is generally helpful to have a service with a regular format, including a clear beginning and end (perhaps lighting and extinguishing a candle with a set form of words). This gives participants a sense of familiarity and security. As discussed in Chapter 10, forms of words with which residents are familiar (for example the KJV) should be used. If you are going to include music, try to gather a portfolio of residents' favourite hymns. You may have a musician on your team, but if not it is possible to get hold of prerecorded organ accompaniments. The only problem is they can be pitched too high. As we age our voices naturally drop in pitch, so confidently led unaccompanied singing at a lower pitch may be preferable. It is also worth preparing shortened versions of hymns (two to three verses are usually enough).

It is wise to take some practical kit with you. Antiseptic hand gel, tissues and a small plastic box for depositing consecrated bread that is discarded or spat out by participants (not an uncommon occurrence) are strongly advisable.

Making connections with local churches

Begin the service by making a connection between this community and the church from which you have come. Say your name (wear a badge with it on too), and name your church and its location in relation to the residence. Bring a postcard or photograph of your church and some of its members. Bring copies of your church newsletter and take copies of the residents' newsletter (if there is one) back to your church in exchange. This will inform the congregation's prayers. If you are an ordained minister it is probably a good idea to wear your clerical shirt and collar; but note that dressing completely in black can frighten some people, and they may wonder if you have come to give the last rites! Even if you are not ordained, you may end up calling yourself 'the vicar' for ease of communication.

If the service involves distributing pre-consecrated bread and wine, make a connection with the time and place that these elements were consecrated. This can be done by saying something like, 'Today is Tuesday. Father John prayed over this bread and wine last Sunday at our morning service. We remembered you then and these come with our love.' (It is good practice to pray for the communities to whom communion will be distributed at some point in the main church service. This makes the ministry more intentional, and connects this part of the community of faith more strongly to the 'centre'.)

Making connections with the world outside

Try to connect residents with the outside world by incorporating news events, birthdays and memorials, and, perhaps most of all, the changing seasons and weather, into your act of worship. People in hospital and residential care have very limited access to fresh outside air. Their environment can feel like a hermetically sealed temperate zone. It may be possible to invite a small group of residents to a special church event such as an afternoon Christmas carol service (but this is often limited by the need for carers to accompany them). If residents can't realistically get out very much, the outside can still be brought in. I once saw this done very beautifully when a worship leader produced some cherry tomatoes from her garden as part of a service with a harvest theme. The participants were each given one. They handled them with great care, enjoying the vibrant colour, the smoothness of the skin and, above all, the complex and evocative fragrance. Then they were offered the opportunity of eating the tomato, which most of them did with great relish.

The outside can also be brought in by having occasional guests, such as a small choir or music group; some children or young people; a well-behaved dog plus owner; or someone from one of the uniformed armed or emergency services (particularly appropriate during the season of Remembrance). *The aim is to remind residents that life is going on and they are still part of it.* One way of getting this across is to have a series of themes through the year. Below is one possible scheme:

- **January:** Turn of the year (snowdrops)
- **February:** Candlemas (candles)
- **March:** Mothering Sunday (spring posies)
- **April:** Easter (Easter eggs or hot cross buns)
- **May:** Carers' thanksgiving (hand massage)
- **June:** Daily bread (cake or bread-making or sharing)
- **July:** Summer holidays (sand and shells)
- **August:** Harvest (fruit and vegetables)
- **September:** Back to school—new beginnings (bulb planting)
- **October:** St Francis and animal blessing (animal visitors)
- **November:** Remembrance (poppies)
- **December:** Advent and Christmas (endless possibilities)

Many residential facilities have a large television in the sitting room. It may be possible to connect this to a laptop and use it to show still pictures or films. These might be of the local church, the local community or landscapes in the general area. Alternatively, pictures that fit the chosen worship theme might be used. It is important not to show too many—just one may be sufficient. An example I have encountered is a very simple meditation based on Psalm 121, which starts 'I lift up my eyes to the hills,' accompanied by photographs of the hills and moors in the vicinity of a particular Scottish care home. This landscape would have been familiar to some of the residents, who were no longer able to enjoy it directly.

Making connections with the Jesus of history and the Christ of faith

Connections go across time as well as space. It is important to connect Christians who are housebound or in residential care with their own faith tradition and the great 'cloud of witnesses' (Hebrews 12:1), through familiar Bible readings, prayers and hymns. Symbols and pictures can be a crucial part of this, especially for those who no longer seem to have language.

Symbolism and story come together in the service of Holy Communion. Here, participants connect deeply with each other, with other Christian communities and with Jesus himself. This happens through the work of the Holy Spirit in an ultimately mysterious way. Nevertheless, we can either set up conditions that allow the Spirit to do his work, or we can put obstacles in the way.

One way to support the connection with Jesus at Holy Communion is by ensuring participants actually hear the story of the Last Supper. This happens automatically at a normal Communion service, where the minister retells the story of Jesus' life, death and resurrection as part of the great prayer of thanksgiving, during which the bread and wine are consecrated. But it is quite likely *not* to happen where pre-consecrated bread and wine are being distributed by others. This is because Jesus' words that the bread was (and is) 'my body, which is given for you' and the wine was (and is) 'my blood… shed for you' are used as part of the prayer of consecration. If the bread and wine have already been consecrated it doesn't feel right to say those words again, and people tend not to.

The unintended consequence of this very common practice[3] is that those who receive Communion at home or in hospital do not hear again the story of the Last Supper, and are effectively disconnected from the historical events from which Holy Communion emerged, and within which it makes sense, and distanced from the One who gave himself 'for you'.

One simple way to remedy this is to include one of the 'institution narratives'[4] as a short Bible reading at an appropriate point in the service. I also always include the 'comfortable words' from the service of Holy Communion in *The Book of Common Prayer*:

> Hear what comfortable words our Saviour Christ saith unto all that truly turn to him.
> Come unto me all that travail and are heavy laden, and I will refresh you. *St Matthew 11:28*

So God loved the world, that he gave his only-begotten Son, to the end that all that believe in him should not perish, but have everlasting life. *St John 3:16*

Networking

Rowan Williams famously said that mission 'is finding out what God is doing and joining in'.[5] This is certainly true in the area of dementia; there is already a lot that churches can join in with going on out there. There are both national and local initiatives. The main charities—The Alzheimer's Society, Age UK, Dementia UK and Young Dementia UK[6]—produce very good information on nearly all aspects of dementia, which can be usefully displayed in churches, especially if those churches are community hubs in their localities. The work of these organisations can be supported through fundraising efforts and monetary giving by churches. Perhaps more importantly, *local churches can get involved in joint initiatives with these and other bodies. A good way of doing this is through a local Dementia Action Alliance (DAA).*[7] These are groups of local organisations that agree to work together to maximise the quality of life for people affected by dementia, through practical and measurable changes in their community. They aim to advance public understanding of dementia; to work in accordance with the views of people affected by dementia; and to report regularly on their progress. In my local community, DAA members include the fire and rescue service, the town council, the Chamber of Commerce, local voluntary societies, the local bus company, pharmacy services, the leisure centre, a local retirement village, and schools and colleges.

It is vital that churches and other faith communities take their place in this sort of enterprise. Church presence is a reminder of the spiritual dimension of human well-being that might otherwise be forgotten. It demonstrates that churches really care about the lives of people affected by dementia, and it showcases the good work churches are already doing. Conversely, churches can learn much from secular organisations to inform their own initiatives and stop themselves reinventing the wheel. Churches often have resources to offer the wider community. For example, they can provide a venue for fundraising, training or publicity events. They can host programmes delivered by others that are directly beneficial to people affected by dementia, such as Singing for the Brain.

This type of networking is a form of blessing, pointing to something wholesome and life-giving, and saying, 'God is here.'[8] It is also a form of witness, because, insofar as churches behave in a way consistent with the nature of God, they witness to his nature. Often this involves affirming the good instincts and aspirations of secular organisations; sometimes it involves challenging their ideas and offering an alternative vision or example of good practice; always it involves service. For the networking of churches with others in their community is not simply a means to a good end—for example, making the community a better place for people affected by dementia. The community *is* its networks. A community built on alliances of goodwill between disparate parties is likely to be more cohesive, just and inclusive—a better community for *all*. It is worth remembering that in his mission to bring in the ultimate friendly community—the kingdom of God—Jesus chose people who were experts with nets and could tolerate different kinds of fish rubbing along together (Matthew 4:18–22; Luke 5:4–10; Matthew 13:47).

Further reading

Malcolm Goldsmith, *In a Strange Land…: People with dementia and the local church* (4M Publications, 2004), Part 3.

Notes

1 www.cqc.org.uk/content/what-does-adult-social-care-look-across-cqcs-new-ratings
2 M. Skrajner et al., 'Training nursing home residents to serve as group activity leaders: Lessons learned and preliminary results from the RAP project', *Dementia*, 11 (2012), pp. 263–74.
3 For example, the Church of England service of 'The distribution of Holy

Communion at home or in hospital' merely alludes to the Last Supper with the words 'The Church of God, of which we are members, has taken bread and wine and given thanks over them according to our Lord's command'. Archbishops' Council, *Common Worship: Pastoral Services* (Church House Publishing, 2000), p. 86.

4 From Matthew 26:26–29; Mark 14:22–25; Luke 22:14–20; or 1 Corinthians 11:23–26.

5 Archbishop's Presidential Address at the General Synod, York, July 2003.

6 www.alzheimers.org.uk; www.ageuk.org.uk; www.dementiauk.org; www.youngdementiauk.org

7 www.dementiaaction.org.uk

8 Recall p. 121.

Chapter 14

Safe enough to play

A community is its networks. Not only do these provide cohesion and strength, they also make the community safer. A healthy community acts as a safety net for its members. A community in which each member looks out for the well-being of others (1 Corinthians 12:24–26), and where the sharing of information and responsibility is the norm, is one where individuals are likely to be safe. The kingdom of God preached by and embodied in Jesus is a place of *shālôm*, a place where 'it's OK' because all have been saved and all are fundamentally safe.

This vision is perhaps most vividly depicted in the book of Zechariah:

> Thus says the Lord of hosts: Old men and old women shall again sit in the streets of Jerusalem, each with staff in hand because of their great age. And the streets of the city shall be full of boys and girls playing in its streets. Thus says the Lord of hosts: Even though it seems impossible to the remnant of this people in these days, should it also seem impossible to me, says the Lord of hosts? Thus says the Lord of hosts: I will save my people from the east country and from the west country; and I will bring them to live in Jerusalem. They shall be my people and I will be their God, in faithfulness and in righteousness.
>
> ZECHARIAH 8:4–8

This is a picture of God's kingdom as a safe place: a place where people can move about freely and play without fear; a place where the weaker and potentially vulnerable are at the centre; and a place where people of all ages, genders and ethnicities are gathered together. It forms a poignant contrast with cities in war zones through the ages.

Most of us do not inhabit war zones, but we live in a world fraught with danger. We are called to participate in the advancement of God's kingdom by making safe spaces for all, especially those who are troubled or vulnerable.

Principles of adult safeguarding

The need to protect children from abuse or neglect started to become part of public consciousness in Britain in the Victorian era, with the first legislation being passed by Parliament in 1889.[1] Awareness of the need to protect vulnerable adults is a much more recent development. A key step occurred with the publication of guidelines by the Department of Health and Home Office in 2000.[2] Significantly, this document was entitled *No Secrets*, and it emphasised the importance of transparent communication and coordinated action by different statutory and voluntary agencies involved with vulnerable adults. Legislation on mental capacity[3] and the regulation of employment for those working with vulnerable adults[4] followed. Many of the recommendations from *No Secrets* were then incorporated into the Care Act of 2014.[5]

The philosophy behind adult safeguarding has a rather different emphasis from that of child safeguarding because it recognises the dangers of inappropriate paternalism and overprotection in dealing with adults. Its aim is to protect adults who are vulnerable due to personal circumstances or the effects of a health condition[6] from abuse or neglect; to support them in making choices about how they want to live; and to promote their overall well-being. There is emphasis on raising awareness of safeguarding among professionals and the general public; on education in recognising signs of abuse and neglect; and on how to respond appropriately if abuse or neglect are suspected.

This philosophy is summed up in six principles:[7]

- Empowerment: people being supported and encouraged to make their own decisions and give informed consent.

- Prevention: it is better to take action before harm occurs.
- Proportionality: the least intrusive response appropriate to the risk presented.
- Protection: support and representation for those in greatest need.
- Partnership: local solutions through services working with their communities.
- Accountability: transparency in delivering safeguarding.

Some of these principles can be in tension with each other. When making decisions in the best interests of the individuals concerned, a balance may need to be struck. For example, an older woman who is at risk from falling may resist a move from her three-storey home into a bungalow because of all the memories associated with her home. The principle of empowerment might lead us to respect that decision; but the principle of protection might lead us to challenge it quite forcefully. In addition, the best interests of one individual might be in tension with the best interests of others—for example, when a person with declining abilities wishes to continue driving. There is also a tension in safeguarding practice between the need for clear communication between interested parties and the need to respect confidentiality and privacy. The relative costs and benefits of different courses of action need to be weighed up, and this can at times feel more like an art than a science.

In making good decisions it is important to have good information and a number of perspectives. This is one reason the Care Act requires agencies to work collaboratively under the supervision of Safeguarding Adults Boards (SABs) in each local area. These SABs are composed of senior representatives from local government, primary healthcare and the police, together with other agencies (such as the ambulance service or user groups) and specialist consultants as appropriate. SABs develop strategies for promoting the well-being and safety of vulnerable adults in their local area, and they have a duty to hold formal reviews of serious cases where a vulnerable adult has died or been in danger of death or serious harm as a result of alleged abuse or neglect.

Specialist safeguarding services are not intended to absolve the whole community of its responsibility, but rather to support and enable it. We can all take steps to safeguard our own interests and the interests of those we love. *On receiving a diagnosis of dementia it is wise to set up a Lasting Power of Attorney*[8] that can be activated in the future when it becomes necessary. *It is also worthwhile considering an Advance Decision.*[9] This is a kind of living will that can be part of an individual's medical care plan. It sets out his or her wishes regarding the use of antibiotics, artificial ventilation, attempts to resuscitate and so on, to be consulted in circumstances when he or she is unable to think clearly or communicate.

Mental capacity and the right to make 'bad choices'

It is natural for us to want to protect children and vulnerable adults from making bad choices in life. The book of Proverbs is full of parental advice about living wisely and avoiding the pitfalls of instant gratification,[10] but it recognises that ultimately the choice of how to live lies with the young adult themselves. This principle is laid out right at the beginning of the Bible in the events of Genesis 3, where God allows Adam and Eve to make a disastrous choice; and it is reworked in the story of the prodigal son, where the father simply stands by as his son embarks on a reckless and self-destructive course of action.

If we are to respect others we must respect their agency and autonomy as far as possible, even when we profoundly disagree with their values and actions. The exception is when harm may be caused to others, or when we believe individuals are 'not in their right mind' or 'do not know what they are doing'. The technical term for this is lack of mental capacity, and the principles for overriding the wishes of those who lack mental capacity, in order to protect their interests or the interests of wider society, are enshrined in the Mental Capacity Act of 2005.

English law has always been clear that doing or wanting to do something stupid is not in itself an indication of mental incapacity:

> An individual should not be regarded as lacking capacity merely because he makes a decision which would not be made by someone of ordinary prudence. Although the law requires an individual to be capable of understanding the nature and effect of a transaction or decision, it does not require him to behave 'in such a manner as to deserve approbation from the prudent, the wise, or the good'.[11]

The Mental Capacity Act also makes it clear that *capacity to make decisions must be presumed and incapacity must be demonstrated*, not the other way around. The capacity to make a decision has to be assessed professionally on a case-by-case basis and on a decision-by-decision basis. This means that at a given time one person with a particular cognitive impairment may have the capacity to decide to get married but not to decide how to spend their money, whereas their friend with a similar cognitive impairment may have the capacity to do neither.

These principles of protecting the liberty of the individual and not presuming incapacity have important implications for people with dementia: *a diagnosis of dementia does not automatically mean that the individual lacks capacity to make all decisions about his life*. If he decides to do something silly this cannot simply be attributed to his condition. He may always have had a propensity to make silly choices, or he may have decided to go a bit mad as, having received a diagnosis of dementia, he feels his days are numbered.

The philosophy behind the Mental Capacity Act invites us, when in doubt, to err on the side of respecting the autonomy of the vulnerable individual rather than of protecting them, and always to act in the way that is least restrictive of their liberty. However, our culture is risk-averse, and there is evidence that healthcare and social care services have tended to act in a paternalistic and overprotective manner in interpreting the act.[12] This valuing of protection above freedom is also a feature of the way our present-day society treats children. As we have seen, one of the disadvantages of receiving a diagnosis of dementia is that the affected individual can come to be perceived primarily as a risk to self or others.

Churches may well need to reflect on their own culture in this light. There is a strong possibility that they will overreact to their history of laxness in safeguarding and become driven by the need to eliminate risk. In reality, risk cannot be entirely eliminated; it can only be managed. Even if a risk-free life were possible, it would be dull. Zechariah's vision of the kingdom is of children at play in the streets. The paradox is that you can't play unless you feel safe (enough), but play is risky.

Behaviour that challenges

A vulnerable adult can herself become a hazard to others if she exhibits 'challenging behaviour'. This term begs the question of who is challenged by the behaviour, and reminds us that sometimes the problem can be with our ability to tolerate healthy distress (recall Chapter 9) rather than the behaviour itself. There is, however, no doubt that behavioural disturbance can be a significant issue for many people with dementia, and can place themselves and others at risk. The sorts of behaviour in question include verbal and physical aggression; shouting and screaming; agitation and restlessness; and socially and sexually offensive conduct. In situations such as that of a frail older man caring for a wife with dementia who is in the habit of hitting out, it is difficult to say which of them is more vulnerable. Family carers of people with dementia admit to a high level of verbal abuse on their part, but this may in turn be a response to abuse at the hands of those for whom they care.[13] *A good approach to safeguarding is to try to work out who the vulnerable individuals in a community actually are, and take the well-being of all these people into account.* In a church community, this will extend to members of the pastoral team who may make themselves vulnerable through their contact with people with a tendency to show challenging behaviour.

However, just as a diagnosis of dementia doesn't automatically mean the affected individual lacks capacity, neither does it automatically mean the affected individual will develop challenging behaviour. Many people with dementia may behave in troubling ways, but many don't, and challenging behaviour is not an inevitable 'symptom' of the condition. Rather, it is a reaction to the situation in which the affected individuals find themselves. If we were in their shoes, or could see the world through their eyes, we might well behave in a similar way. The primary problem is usually with the way individuals experience their world; their behaviour is secondary to this. It follows that the best approach to challenging behaviour is to help them experience their world differently.

It is always worth asking some simple questions when a person with dementia develops inexplicable or challenging behaviour. The place to start is with her experience of her inner physical world. Does she need the toilet? Is she in pain, or thirsty, or hungry, or running a temperature? Does attending to these needs make a difference to the behaviour? The next thing to consider is the immediate environment. Is the level of stimulation appropriate? Is it too hot, too cold, too noisy or too bright? Does varying the environment make a difference to the behaviour?

If these simple approaches do not work, the next step is to ask some questions about the person's mental world. Are they experiencing troubling mental events such as hallucinations? This is one case where medication may help. More commonly, dealing with the individual's mental world will mean trying to enter it (Chapter 7), and seeing whether the behaviour has arisen because they are misreading the situation. For example, a gentleman with dementia once caused a good deal of distress and embarrassment to his family, because when home-care staff arrived to get him up in the morning he would remove his pyjama bottoms and make sexual advances to them. It is true that the pattern of his brain fade meant his ability to control his impulses was somewhat reduced, but the main driver of this behaviour was the way he saw the world. Two attractive young women of Asian ethnicity arrived in his bedroom and began to undress him while he was still half asleep; he concluded that he was on holiday and unfortunately that these were foreign sex workers, and he responded accordingly. In this case, his challenging behaviour was managed by his long-suffering care staff changing the timing of the visits; changing the approach from friendly and open to cooler and more professional; and by providing him with continuous, clear commentary about the nature of this encounter.

When it comes to aggressive behaviour, the most common causes are not damage to the 'aggression centres of the brain', but being asked to do something too difficult, frustration at not being able to communicate and—above all—fear. Recall that people with Alzheimer's and related conditions can learn to be afraid but cannot reason their way out of it. This may be compounded if the person misinterprets the situation in the light of old memories, for example thinking a nurse is in fact a prison guard. We respond to fear by trying to avoid or escape from the thing that frightens us. Often this is simply by saying, 'No!' If you can no longer slam the door, run away or speak, or if others ignore your verbal protests, then you are likely to resort to physical resistance. It is a good rule of thumb to assume most people with advanced dementia are afraid, and to treat them as if they are—speaking quietly, moving slowly and touching gently, with warning.

Sometimes the challenging behaviour is an attempt to communicate a significant desire, such as the need to get home or, as in the case of Jack from Chapter 7, for the cows to be in. A lady resident in a care home called loudly for her mother at sunset every day. On one occasion, instead of giving her the usual response that her mother was long dead and would not be coming, a member of staff asked, 'What would your mum do if she was here?' The lady replied, 'She would pull down the blackout blinds.' It became clear that the lady was anxious about becoming an air-raid target. The member of staff shut the curtains and the problem was solved. Of course, things are not always that easy, but the principle of trying to access the affected individual's reality will always be important.

One serious reason for the development of challenging or withdrawn behaviour in a vulnerable person who has previously been on a relatively even keel is the occurrence of abuse, to which we now turn.

Safe from harm

Abuse can be understood as the violation of an individual's human or civil rights, by causing harm[14] through active perpetration or passive neglect. It may be intentional, done in ignorance or accidental. Some people are uncomfortable with the language of rights and prefer the idea of needs,[15] but all agree that a decent society should ensure its most vulnerable members are suitably fed, clothed and housed; kept clean; protected from harm; connected with others; and helped to live their lives to the full with dignity and an appropriate degree of freedom.

Various types of abuse are recognised. The most obvious are physical and sexual abuse, but there are other more subtle forms, and people with dementia are potentially vulnerable to them all.

- **Physical abuse** includes hitting; slapping; pushing; kicking; misuse of medication; restraint; and inappropriate sanctions.

- **Sexual abuse** includes rape and sexual assault; and sexual acts to which the vulnerable adult has not consented or could not consent, or was pressured into consenting to.

- **Psychological abuse** includes emotional abuse; threats of harm or abandonment; deprivation of contact; humiliation; blaming; controlling; intimidation; coercion; harassment; verbal abuse; isolation; and withdrawal from services or supportive networks.

- **Financial or material abuse** includes theft; fraud; exploitation; pressure in connection with wills, property or inheritance, or financial transactions; and the misuse or misappropriation of property, possessions or benefits.

- **Neglect and acts of omission** include ignoring medical or physical care needs; failure to provide access to appropriate healthcare or social care services; and withholding the necessities of life, such as medication, adequate nutrition and heating.

- **Discriminatory abuse** may take the form of any of the above categories, but is motivated and aggravated by discriminatory attitudes to the individual's race, gender, sexuality, religion, age, disability and so on. It will usually include verbal slurs that make this clear.

- **Institutional abuse** refers to a situation in which a whole system colludes with abusive attitudes and practices; in which the running of an institution is for the benefit of staff rather than clients or residents; and in which allegations receive inadequate responses because clients or residents are viewed as problematic.

Responding to abuse

There are four ways in which you may encounter abuse: you may be caught up in it as perpetrator or victim (we will not pursue this one further here); you may witness it; you may see signs such as bruises or behaviour changes that lead you to suspect it; or an individual may disclose it to you.

The first and most important principle is to make the situation safe, or at least not to make it any more dangerous. When you witness an acute and clear incident of abuse, contact the police. When a vulnerable individual discloses abuse, take care not to confront or alert the alleged perpetrator before arrangements can be made to make the victim safe (for example, in the case of a person who alleges abuse by their spouse, who is also their main carer and with whom they share their home).

The second principle is to preserve evidence by making a written record and, where necessary, taking photographs. When an individual discloses abuse, listen calmly and encourage her to tell her story, but do not lead her in a particular direction. Do this by using neutral phrases such as 'Tell me…', 'Explain to me…' and 'Describe to me…' Accept what you have been told, not by making value judgments such as 'What he did was outrageous!' but in more measured terms, for example, 'What you have told me is really important.' Do not promise to keep the disclosure secret. The privacy of the alleged victim needs to be respected, but you must be free to share information appropriately on a need-to-know basis, and always with your supervisor or mentor.

The third principle is to maintain the trust of the person who has disclosed abuse, or who you suspect is being abused, by keeping him informed of the action you intend to take and, where possible, obtaining his consent. However, consent to share information is not necessary if you judge the vulnerable adult concerned to be at ongoing, significant risk of harm. This can often require delicate judgment, and you should always consult with your supervisor in such cases.

The fourth principle is to ensure you have an accountability relationship with someone with whom you can discuss the issue, and who can give you advice, supervision and support. This is merely good pastoral practice and should be the norm in church pastoral care teams.[16] Of course, you may not have any sort of pastoral role, but may simply stumble upon abuse in your place of work or in the community. You may nevertheless want to turn to your church for advice and support. In this case, your church safeguarding officer would be the first port of call.

The fifth principle is to report abuse to the appropriate authority. If a disclosure happens or your suspicions are aroused in the context of your church or concerning church members, then the safeguarding officer for your congregation or group of churches should be informed.

If you are unsure who to tell, or whether the alleged incident really merits reporting, contact your local SAB for advice. Another possibility is to talk to the individual's GP. When a care home is involved, the Care Quality Commission (CQC) can be helpful.[17]

A safe-enough church

Each church needs to have an agreed, formal safeguarding policy. This does not have to be written from scratch; the main Christian denominations have national[18] and local[19] guidelines. Not only should the policy identify individuals who will take the lead on safeguarding and be trained accordingly,[20] it also needs to promote awareness of safeguarding across the whole congregation. The policy should include a section on recruiting volunteers, especially those who are likely to work alone with vulnerable adults, and clarification on which roles require a Disclosure and Barring Service (DBS) check.[21]

It is a good idea to carry out a regular risk assessment of the church's physical environment, in terms of lighting, trip hazards and so on, but also with the aim of making the environment positively friendly rather than simply low risk (see Chapter 10). Risk management also involves taking care of those who are involved in pastoral ministry. When our memory starts to fail we have a tendency to blame others. Sometimes this is fairly harmless—'Why are you hiding my spectacles?'—but sometimes it is more serious—'Who took the £50 I had in my purse?' The whole point about dementia is that its onset is gradual and insidious. A longstanding congregation member may appear to be behaving in line with his generous character when he makes a large donation to the organ fund, but it is vital to be alert to possible changes in capacity in such cases. Is the decision a considered one? Will he remember it next month? Is the church at risk of accusations of defrauding him? Meticulous record keeping and good communication are vital in such circumstances.

On a smaller scale, helping someone out with shopping may become more hazardous as her memory begins to decline and she forgets whether she gave you a £5 or a £20 note. Again, meticulous record keeping will be key to managing this situation. It is also wise to share pastoral care of an individual across a team, and at least with one other person who can be a source of support, provide an alternative perspective and be a witness to events. Jesus' example of sending his disciples out in pairs is one we should fully embrace for all sorts of reasons.

Keeping our own notes of pastoral encounters can also be seen as a way of bearing witness to proceedings. It will become standard practice in most churches in the future, although the precise way it is done will vary depending on local circumstances. The simplest format is a notebook in which to record the date and time of an encounter (such as a visit or conversation) that could be described as pastoral. The notes should specify where the encounter took place and who was present, and include a brief sentence on the nature of the encounter. For example:

> Wednesday 20 May 2016—visited Mrs Smith at home at her request to give her Holy Communion. Her daughter, Fran, was present in the house but did not take part in the service. (Signed...)

Obviously, had Mrs Smith complained during the visit that Fran was taking her money, then the notes would be much more detailed and include some sort of action plan.

These sorts of records should be kept in a secure place and treated as the property of the church rather than the individual. The specific procedure for making and storing the records (paper or electronic) should be part of the safeguarding policy of the church. This may seem an overly bureaucratic approach to pastoral care, especially in view of the discussion earlier in this chapter on tolerating risk. In fact, it is a way of making pastoral care more intentional, considered and significant. It treats it with the seriousness it deserves. Such notes can be a prompt to prayer, and can also take 'thinking of you' to a deeper level, acting as a record when memory of the pastoral encounter starts to fade. They are, with all their limitations, a way of re-membering the person.

Further reading

Joanna Collicutt McGrath, *Ethical Practice in Brain Injury Rehabilitation* (Oxford University Press, 2007), Chapters 4 and 6.

Michael Mandelstam, *Safeguarding Adults and the Law* (Jessica Kingsley, 2013).

Michael Paterson and Jessica Rose (eds), *Enriching Ministry: Pastoral supervision in practice* (SCM Press, 2014).

June Andrews, *Dementia: The one-stop guide* (Profile Books, 2015), Chapter 8.

Notes

1 Prevention of Cruelty to, and Protection of, Children Act 1889.

2 Department of Health and Home Office, *No Secrets: Guidance on developing and implementing multi-agency policies and procedures to protect vulnerable adults from abuse* (Department of Health, 2000): www.gov.uk/government/uploads/system/uploads/attachment_data/file/194272/No_secrets__guidance_on_developing_and_implementing_multi-agency_policies_and_procedures_to_protect_vulnerable_adults_from_abuse.pdf

3 Mental Capacity Act 2005: www.legislation.gov.uk/ukpga/2005/9/contents

4 Safeguarding Vulnerable Groups Act 2006: www.legislation.gov.uk/ukpga/2006/47/section/59

5 Care Act 2014, Section 14: www.legislation.gov.uk/ukpga/2014/23/contents/enacted/data.htm

6 In practice this is likely to be someone with a mental health condition such as schizophrenia; a physical health condition such as diabetes; cognitive impairment arising from a condition such as autism or dementia; physical impairment arising from a condition such as cerebral palsy or spinal-cord injury; drug or alcohol dependency; sensory impairment; or restricted liberty due to imprisonment for a criminal offence or detention under the Mental Health Act or the Immigration and Asylum Act.

7 Department of Health, *Care and Support Statutory Guidance: Issued under the Care Act 2014* (Williams Lea, 2014), p. 232.

8 Useful information on this is available from Age UK: tel: 0800 169 2081; www.ageuk.org.uk/money-matters/legal-issues/powers-of-attorney/lasting-power-of-attorney

9 More information on Advance Decisions is available from Compassion in Dying: tel: 0800 999 2434; www.compassionindying.org.uk

10 For example, Proverbs 23.

11 Bird v. Luckie (1850); 8 Hare 301.

12 HM Government, *Valuing Every Voice, Respecting Every Right: Making the Case for the Mental Capacity Act: The Government's response to the House of Lords Select Committee Report on the Mental Capacity Act 2005* (Williams Lea, 2014). www.gov.uk/government/uploads/system/uploads/attachment_data/file/318730/cm8884-valuing-every-voice.pdf

13 A. Wiglesworth et al., 'Screening for abuse and neglect of people with dementia', *Journal of the American Geriatrics Society,* 58 (2010), pp. 493–500.

14 *No Secrets*, p. 9.

15 Abraham Maslow's famous 'hierarchy of needs' is relevant here. He lists these as physiological, safety, love and belonging, esteem, self-actualisation and self-transcendence needs. A. Maslow, 'A theory of human motivation', *Psychological Review*, 50 (1943), pp. 370–96.

16 The Association for Pastoral Supervision and Education is a useful resource here: www.pastoralsupervision.org.uk

17 The CQC is the independent regulator of health and social care in England: www.cqc.org.uk; CQC National Customer Service Centre, Citygate, Gallowgate, Newcastle upon Tyne, NE1 4PA; tel: 03000 616161. This is for England only. The role and scope of regulatory bodies in other parts of the UK are not identical to that of the CQC.

18 For example, the House of Bishops' guidance: *Promoting a Safe Church: Policy for safeguarding adults in the Church of England* (Church House Publishing, 2006): www.churchofengland.org/media/37405/promotingasafechurch.pdf

19 For example, Diocese of Oxford, *Safeguarding Handbook for the Protection of Children and Vulnerable Adults* (2012): www.oxford.anglican.org/wp-content/uploads/2013/02/safeguarding_handbook.pdf

20 Helpful advice on training is available from the Churches' Child Protection Advisory Service (CCPAS), which also covers adult safeguarding: www.ccpas.co.uk; PO Box 133, Swanley, Kent, BR8 7UQ; tel: 01322 517817.

21 The procedures vary between England and Wales, and Scotland, and Northern Ireland. See www.gov.uk/disclosure-barring-service-check/overview

BRF

Transforming
lives and communities

Christian growth and understanding of the Bible

Resourcing individuals, groups and leaders in churches for their
own spiritual journey and for their ministry

Church outreach in the local community

Offering three programmes that churches are embracing
to great effect as they seek to engage
with their local communities
and transform lives

Teaching Christianity in primary schools

Working with children and teachers to explore Christianity
creatively and confidently

Children's and family ministry

Working with churches and families to explore Christianity
creatively and bring the Bible alive

Visit **brf.org.uk** for more information on BRF's work
Review this book on Twitter using **#BRFconnect**

brf.org.uk